S0-BTC-840

COLOSSIANS
and
PHILEMON:
A Runaway Church and a Runaway Slave

Jim Townsend

DAVID C. COOK PUBLISHING CO.
ELGIN, ILLINOIS • WESTON, ONTARIO

PERSONAL LIBRARY
Of Mark Henderson

To Lucy . . .
whose love lights up my life.

Colossians and Philemon: A Runaway Church and a Runaway Slave
© 1987 by David C. Cook Publishing Co.

All rights reserved. Except for brief excerpts for review purposes, no part of this book may be reproduced or used in any form without written permission from the publisher.

Scripture taken from the HOLY BIBLE, NEW INTERNATIONAL VERSION. ©1973, 1978, 1984 International Bible Society. Used by permission of Zondervan Bible Publishers.

David C. Cook Publishing Co.
850 North Grove Avenue
Elgin, IL 60120
Printed in U.S.A.

Editor: Gary Wilde
Designer: Dawn Lauck
Cover: Bakstad Photographics

ISBN: 1-55513-849-7
Library of Congress Catalog Number: 87-70309

CONTENTS

INTRODUCTION

Welcome to the Bible Mastery Series, designed to aid serious Bible students in group settings. Ideally, every student should have a copy of this study manual. Then the group sessions will be spent focusing largely upon the questions and activities at the back of the book in the DIRECTIONS FOR GROUP LEADERS section, p. 130. **Since all participants should have read the up-front commentary before class, the group's time can be spent primarily upon sharing experiences about how to apply these truths to their lives (rather than in factual and interpretive discussions).**

Each chapter contains many quotes and ideas from the best of past and present evangelical scholarship. In effect, I have provided a mini-library of information from the standard, solid commentators that Bible students turn to for interpretation and explanation. In most cases, the Notes section at the back of the book will give sources for the information. I did the digging; you get the results!

The Symbols

Various boxes are set off from the rest of the text. These will give background information or illustration from such areas as theology, archaeology, original languages, etc. Here is a key to the symbols:

 GREEKSPEAK: Concise explanations of important Greek words, tenses, syntax, to help with interpreting the text's meaning.

 THEOLOGITALK: Discusses theological terms and doctrinal issues in relation to the text.

 CAN YOU DIG IT? Gives valuable cultural insight from archaeology.

 QUOTABLE QUOTES: Memorable statements from various sources.

 WINDOW ON THE WORD: Anecdotal material to illustrate a point in the text.

 THOUGHT QUESTION: A chance to pause and reflect on issues raised in the text.

OUTLINES OF COLOSSIANS AND PHILEMON

Before jumping right into the verses of Colossians and Philemon you will want to soar above them to get a panoramic sweep of each entire book.

COLOSSIANS
I. *Opening Greetings and Gratitude (1:1-11)*
  A. The Greetings He Relays (1:1, 2)
  B. The Gratitude He Relates (1:3-8)
  C. The Goals He Requests (1:9-11)

II. *A Theology to Treasure (1:12—2:7)*
  A. The Shift to Reconciliation (1:12-14)
  B. The Hymn Celebrating Reconciliation (1:15-20)
  C. The Colossians Involved in Reconciliation—as object (1:21-23a)
  D. Paul Involved in Reconciliation—as subject (1:23b—2:5)

III. *A Life-Style to Live (2:8—4:6)*
  A. Not Based on False "Philosophy" (2:8-15)
  B. Not Regulated by Ascetic Regulations (2:16—3:4)
  C. Characterized by Heaven-on-Earth Character (3:5-17)
  D. Practiced in Down-to-Earth Relationships (3:18—4:1)
  E. Supported by Prayerful Wisdom (4:2-6)

IV. *Closing Greetings and Grace (4:7-18)*
  A. Two Letter Carriers (4:7-9):
    Tychicus and Onesimus
  B. Three Jewish Stalwarts (4:10, 11):
    Aristarchus, Mark, and Jesus Justus
  C. Three Gentile Co-Workers (4:12-14):
    Epaphras, Luke, and Demas
  D. Two Local Christians (4:15-17):
    Nympha and Archippus

PHILEMON
I. *Greetings (Saying "Hi")—1-3*
II. *Gratitude (Saying "Thanks")—4-7*
III. *Appeal (Speaking softly)—8-22*
IV. *Addendum (Saying "So long")—23-25*

CHAPTER
1

LET'S GET INTRODUCED
Colossians 1:1-8

Did you ever thrill as a child to tales of swashbuckling buccaneers, gold doubloons, and adventures on the high seas? In Robert Louis Stevenson's *Treasure Island*, young Jim Hawkins boards the good ship *Hispaniola* in quest of buried treasure. Captain Billy Bones's sea chest has yielded a map with a red X containing the words "Bulk of treasure here." This spurs a crew of sailors onward in search of buried wealth.

Christians possess a similar treasure-laden document in Colossians. Colossians 2:3 is the "red-X verse" labeled "Bulk of treasure here." In Christ "are hidden all the treasures of wisdom and knowledge." Christians are rightly entitled to the treasure, for "the Father . . . has qualified you to share in the inheritance . . . in the kingdom of light.

GNOSSUS OF COLOSSUS SAYS...

DON'T YOU JUST LOVE FINDING BURIED TREASURE?

For he has rescued us from the dominion of darkness and brought us into the kingdom of the Son he loves" (Col. 1:12, 13).

Nevertheless, as *Treasure Island* had its mutinous pirates collaborating with Long John Silver, so at Colosse there was a crew of philosophical pirates out to plunder those sailing under the Christian flag. The expression "takes you captive" (in Col. 2:8) is used in Greek literature outside the Bible for carrying off booty, or for kidnapping. Thus, "the glorious riches of this mystery, which is Christ" (Col. 1:27) must be guarded.

Before tackling a verse-by-verse study of the book of Colossians, let's look at the background of this book. Just as we might better understand the furniture a person selected in light of the decor of the rooms of a house, looking at the overall "decor" at Colosse will aid us in understanding the individual decorations. Look up the Bible verses and fill in the blanks:

Blanks in the Background

On his third missionary journey, Paul spent _____ years teaching in the school of _____ in the city of _____ (Acts 19:1, 9, 10). Paul spent a total of _____ years at Ephesus (Acts 20:31). Ephesus, a few miles inland on the west coast of Asia Minor, was located in the Roman province of _____ (Acts 19:10).

About one hundred miles from Ephesus (on the main east-west highway) were the tri-cities of _____ , _____ , and _____ (Col. 1:2; 4:13), located in southwest _____ (Acts 18:23, the second region named.) Colosse was about ten miles southeast of _____ (Col. 4:15) and thirteen miles southerly from _____ (Col 4:13). These cities formed a triangle. From Col. 2:1 one might gather that the Colossian believers had _____ _____ Paul _____ . Rather than Paul, _____ (Col. 1:7) of the city of _____ (Col. 4:12;1:2) seems to have founded the Colossian church. Perhaps he carried the Christian message from Ephesus back to the Lycus (Wolf) River district, where Colosse lay.

Epaphras had been a _____ _____ (Philem. 23) with Paul, probably in _____ (Acts 28:14), where for _____ years Paul was held prisoner in his own _____ _____ (Acts 28:30). Epaphras had reported the threat of a false _____ (Col. 2:8) at Colosse to Paul (Col. 1:7, 8), who was in _____ (Col. 4:18). During his first Roman imprisonment Paul probably wrote Ephesians, Philippians, Colossians, and Philemon (the Prison Epistles). From Col. 4:7-9 we learn that _____ and _____ were the mail carriers who brought this letter to Colosse.

Geography

Take a few moments to study the map above of Asia Minor. (If you need to set it in its larger context, get out an atlas or globe and find the bigger spot into which you would fit this piece of the geographical puzzle.) After studying the map, see if you can put it aside, draw the fist shaped Asia Minor, and label on it the locations of the cities of Ephesus, Colosse, Laodicea, and Hierapolis.

The Meander River meandered its way across Asia Minor, and its tributary, the Lycus River, ran between Hierapolis (on the north) and Colosse (on the south). Colosse was populated with native Phrygians, Greeks, and Jewish colonists.

History

Colosse's heyday was past when Paul wrote. In the fifth century B.C. the Greek historian Herodotus, chronicling Xerxes and the Persian army's march to Thermopylae, called Colosse a "great city." Another Greek writer, Xenophon, commented on its civic prosperity about 80 years after Herodotus. Still later, Pliny the Elder, a Roman writer, dubbed Colosse one of the most famous cities of Phrygia. However, around the beginning of the Christian calendar, the Greek geographer Strabo referred to it as a small town. As a city, then, Colosse was among the least important to which Paul wrote letters. It was moving into its sunset years when Paul penned this letter to some of its citizens. In fact, it is never named in the Book of Acts. The city was destroyed by an earthquake during the emperor Nero's reign. Interestingly, Colosse has never been seriously excavated.

Date

Many believe Paul wrote two sets of letters from Roman prisons: (1) the four Prison Epistles (Ephesians, Philippians, Colossians, Philemon); and (2) the three Pastoral Epistles (I and II Timothy, Titus). Although he wore chains (Col. 4:18), Paul seems to have enjoyed more freedom during the first Roman imprisonment (Acts 28:16, 20, 23, 30, 31). During the second Roman imprisonment, tradition places him in the Mamertine Prison.

Many scholars date the writing of Colossians (along with Ephesians, Philippians, and Philemon) between A.D. 60 and 63. Any side-by-side reading of Ephesians beside Colossians reveals that much of their texture is drawn from the same bolt of cloth. In fact, about 25% of Colossians is found in Ephesians. Yet Colossians and Ephesians are not quite identical twins, for Colossians is targeted for a much more specific situation than Ephesians.

 Can you name the four Prison Epistles and the three Pastoral Epistles? About what date may Paul have written Colossians?

Purpose

Why was Colossians written? The purpose in penning Colossians was (1) polemical and (2) pastoral or positive. *Polemical* comes from a Greek word for "battle," and it means that Paul had to combat and counterattack a controversial cult. It was as if there were some enemy submarine slinking around right off shore.

Still, Colossians is much more than a combat document. The polemical purpose is couched within an overall positive purpose. Therefore, Paul proclaims a Christ above all and a Christianity for all.

THE CONTROVERSIAL CULT AT COLOSSE

Reading between the lines of Colossians helps us reconstruct why Colossians was written and what the controversy behind the book was all about. Colossians must be approached somewhat in the spirit of a "whodunit." Who were the villains, as it were, lurking behind the curtains in the Colossian drama? Point for point, they are not precisely like any ancient cult we know. That is why many Bible scholars simply call this the "Colossian heresy."

Nevertheless, there are striking similarities between the cult at

Colosse and a second-century group known as the Gnostics (NAHS-ticks). An *agnostic* is one claiming "not (to) know" whether there is a God. Hence, a *Gnostic* was one who staked claim to special hidden knowledge: "I *do* know." Just as an amateur dressmaker may match a patch of polka-dotted material against a larger piece to make an exact identification, even so we can identify the cult at Colosse by comparing it with what came later. What is found in seed form at Colosse about A.D. 63 appeared in full flower a hundred years later as Gnosticism.

How does one explain evil? That was Gnosticism's principal question. To the Gnostic, the material world was intrinsically evil. Someone has quipped that the way to understand Gnosticism is by asking, "What's the matter with our world?" The answer is: "Matter (i.e., all items of a physical makeup) is what's the matter." Once one has grasped this idea—that anything physical is evil in and of itself—one has understood the main plank in the Gnostic way of thinking.

The above principle is like a two-story view of life: everything spiritual is automatically good, and everything material is automatically evil. (Before proceeding further, see if you can guess how such a life view would affect Christianity.) One with Gnostic assumptions viewed with a different lens: (1) the way God must relate to our world, (2) the kind of makeup Jesus must have, and (3) the kind of life-style one should live. Let's examine each of these.

First, if spirit is good and matter is evil, how could a God (spirit) make any contact with our world (matter) without contamination? To solve this problem, Gnostics came up with a ladderlike scheme of beings, called emanations or aeons, who would operate between a spiritual deity and a material world. The New English Bible translates Colossians 2:20 as reflecting this chain of beings. Venerating these "elemental spirits of the universe," who were thought to control human destiny, amounted to a "worship of angels" (Col. 2:18). But by His death, Christ "disarmed the [spiritual] powers and authorities" (Col. 2:15) of any imagined engineering of human destinies.

Secondly, if spirit is good and matter is evil, how could Jesus ever possess a real human body? The Gnostic answer was: He just *appeared* to have a body (a *docetic* view of Christ, from the Greek word *dokeo*, meaning "to appear," "to seem." Consequently, Edgar Goodspeed called these cultists "Seemists."). By the same token, a bodily resurrection would be pointless, for Greeks believed generally in the immortality of the soul but not the resurrection of the body. This view is capsuled neatly by a two-word Greek poem: *soma sema*. *Soma* is Greek for "body," and *sema* means "prison." For Greeks the body was a prison to escape from and not to be desired in the afterlife.

Thirdly, if spirit is good and matter is evil, how should people treat their bodies? Strangely, two diametrically opposite reactions cropped up. Some said, "Be indulgent with your body. Live it up." Others said, "Be indifferent to your body." The first group became pleasure-seeking *antinomians* (those living lawlessly). The second group became *ascetics* (mirrored in "their harsh treatment of the body," Col. 2:23).

Take a moment to consider some modern counterparts to the Gnostic notions. (Perhaps you can add some of your own entries.)

1. Mind over matter advocates, who spiritualize earthly realities as Gnostics feared to contaminate God by any direct contact with the physical world.
2. Scientology, with its emphasis upon the mind, just as Gnostics stressed a special *gnosis (KNOW-sis)*, "knowledge," known only to a select few. The Colossian heresy was a "first century scientology."[1]
3. Horoscope fatalism—regulating human existence by the stars (or powers behind the material elements), as the cult at Colosse apparently held that the "elemental spirits of the universe" (Col. 2:20, NEB) governed their lives.
4. Psychological determinism—e.g., "My mother is responsible for the way I act; I can't do anything about it," as the ancients felt caught in the grip of powers beyond them before Christ "disarmed the powers" (Col. 2:15).
5. Fun-firsters—e.g., the deejay who advocates, "Live it up, but not so much that you can't live it down" (Col. 3:5).
6. Killjoys who engage in "harsh treatment of the body" (Col. 2:23), but who fail to recognize that "God . . . richly provides us with everything for our enjoyment" (I Tim. 6:17).

Such ideas are viewed by Paul as philosophical piracy. He raises the cry, "Walk the plank!"

FOR OPENERS

Seafaring souls would be familiar with Poseidon, the mythical Greek god of the sea (called Neptune by the Romans). Usually Poseidon is pictured with a trident—an oversized, three-pronged pickle fork. Like Poseidon's trident, Colossians 1:1-14 begins with three prongs:

1. Greetings from Paul (1:1, 2);
2. Gratitude for their productivity (1:3-8);
3. Goals and gratitude expressed by Paul in prayer (1:9-14).

Not only will we suggest a three-pronged pickle fork to outline the first 14 verses, but every salutation (the word Bible scholars usually use for Paul's openers) Paul penned also had three prongs. Our modern letters have conventional opening formulas (return address in the upper right-hand corner, "Dear Mr. Cruse," etc.). Likewise, Paul used the conventional letter opening of his own day. For instance, notice the structural underpinnings of a secular letter-opening in Acts 23:25, 26:

A. "Claudius Lysias,
B. "To His Excellency, Governor Felix":
C. "Greetings" (*chairein*—pronounced *KAI-rain*— in Greek).

Now compare the salutation in James 1:1:
A. "James, a servant," etc.;
B. "To the twelve tribes," etc.;
C. "Greetings" (*chairein*).

Next, compare Paul's opener in Colossians 1:1, 2:
A. "Paul, an apostle," etc.;
B. "To the . . . brothers . . . in Colosse";
C. "Grace and peace to you . . . ."

In all three of these cases we observe the same structural features or stylized format:
A. Author (writer);
B. Addressees (or readers);
C. Address (opening greeting).

 Is there any lesson to be learned simply from the way Paul opens his letters? I.e., by the fact that he uses the basic format any non-Christian might use?

For a Christian to be "not of the world" (Jn. 17:16) does not mean being weird, off the wall, or that we have to act differently about everything we do. Just because many non-Christians wear blue jeans does not mean that to be "not of the world" Christians must therefore avoid wearing blue jeans. Just as Paul picked up the standard letter writing formula of his day, and Martin Luther and Charles Wesley borrowed secular tunes to use with Christian hymn lyrics, even so there are many neutral media or items that Christians may adopt for their use. However, not only did Paul *adopt* this secular letter-opening formula, also he *adapted* the manner (or format) to the matter (or the content). Ordinarily Greek writers began with "Greetings" (see Acts 23:26; Jas. 1:1). By spiritual chemistry Paul transformed ordinary

13

"Greetings" (*chairein*) into extraordinary "Grace" (*charis*). It was a word loaded with Christian charm for him, expressing the sheer generosity of God to sinking humanity. From the Greek word *charis* (the *ch* is pronounced with a hard *k*-sound) we derive the English nouns "charity" and "charm."

? What do our English words "charity" and "charm" tell us about God's grace?

Salvation really is heaven's handout. All of us come to God by means of celestial charity or spiritual welfare. Dr. James Crichton defined grace theologically as the "sheer generosity of God flowing downward to undeserving, ill-deserving, hell-deserving sinners." Grace is always God condescending (II Cor. 8:9) to this rebel race. Since Paul, who had gone A.W.O.L. from God, had experienced this amazing grace (I Tim. 1:13-15; especially vs. 14), it became a favorite word in his letters. We might even call "grace" Paul's trademark, monogram, or logo.

The average person in the Greek-speaking world of Paul's day would greet you in the street with *chairein* ("greetings" or "rejoice," as in Jas. 1:1). The average Jew's street greeting was *shalom* ("peace").

? Can any lesson be learned by the way Paul adopts and adapts forms of these greeting words used by Greeks and Jews?

In essence, Paul had captured the best of both worlds. He *adopted* the Jews' "peace" (conveying the ideas of wholeness, wellness, integratedness—something modern psychologists promote). Furthermore, Paul *adapted* the Greek "hello" by elevating it into something supernatural ("grace"). Thus, Paul, as it were, had invaded both worlds (Jew and Gentile) with Christian cargo.

Who is this person who accosts all alike with greetings imported from beyond? This was no less than the man called "the hunting leopard of Pharisaism."[2] By what right does Paul write? He is "an apostle of Christ Jesus by the will of God" (1:1). At root "apostle" and "missionary" have the same meaning. When asked the meaning of a missionary, a child pulled out a penny and said, "one sent." Like a torpedo or missile being launched by superhuman power, Paul was a special brand of missionary commissioned by Christ in harmony with God's master plan. What lessons can one learn by seeing a relationship between the terms "missionary," "commissioned," and "missile" (from the same root)? In the chart on the next page, see how many parallels you can name between an apostle and a missile.

14

APOSTLE | MISSILE

 The term "apostle" is found 28 times in Acts and 38 times in the Epistles. Various individuals or groups in the New Testament receive the nametag of "apostle." Below are listed some of the different usages.
1. The Twelve (Lk. 6:13; 9:10)
2. Paul (Col. 1:1; Gal. 1:11, 12; I Cor. 9:1)
3. Church messengers (II Cor. 8:23; Phil. 2:25 in Greek)
4. Other individuals (Barnabas in Acts 14:4, 14; Andronicus and Junias in Rom. 16:7).

Two principal qualifications for apostles are listed in Acts 1:21, 22. First, miracles were "mark[s of] an apostle" (II Cor. 12:12). Like missiles detonated with special power, the apostles were empowered with divine dynamic. Second, apostles are depicted (in Eph. 2:20, for instance) as part of the "foundation" of the Christian Church.

Paul's understudy was Timothy (Col. 1:1). Timothy is named 24 times in the New Testament. He is co-named with Paul in six of the openings of his Epistles. Timothy, the product of a hybrid marriage (Acts 16:1), had been steeped in the Scriptures by his mother and grandmother since early childhood (II Tim. 1:5; 3:15). He had become a Christian during Paul's first missionary journey and traveled with Paul on his second missionary journey. During the third missionary journey, when Timothy was with Paul in Ephesus, some of the people from Colosse probably came to hear Paul—and met Timothy, too. Timothy seems to have spent some time in prison (Heb. 13:23).

The readers are members of two worlds, citizens of two circles.

To be "in Christ," said David Allen (in a 1983 radio sermon), is like being "in an elevator"—there is no half-way spot; you're either inside or you're not.

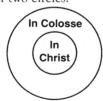

After the greetings (vss. 1:1, 2) comes the gratitude (vss. 1:3-8). Actually, Colossians 1:3-8

is a single sentence, a typical example of Paul's penchant for stringing words together without actual sentence breaks. Chapter one has only five sentences in the original Greek language, one of which contains 218 words. We can see some sense of structure if we peruse the diagram below. Note the matching parts.

Thanksgiving—Beyond a Holiday
Colossians 1:3-12

We . . . thank God (*eucharistoumen*), vs. 3
   when we pray for you (*proseuchomenoi peri humon*), vs. 3
      because we . . . heard (*akousantes*), vs. 4
         of the love (*agapen*), vs. 4
      you have already heard (*proekousate*), vs. 5
         as (*kathos*)—vs. 6
           [as] (*kathos*)—vs. 7
      since the day you heard (*ekousate*), vs. 6
         your love (*agapen*) in the Spirit, vs. 8
      since the day we heard, vs. 9 (*ekousamen*)
   praying for you (*proseuchomenoi huper humon*), vs. 9
giving thanks (*eucharistountes*), vs. 12

Here is the way one ancient, non-Christian Greek letter opens: "Apion to Epimachus his father and lord, many greetings (*chairein*). . . . I thank the Lord Serapis that, when I was in peril in the sea, he saved me . . . ."[3]

 What similarities does Paul's opening Thanksgiving show in common with the non-Christian one quoted above?

Sometimes pseudospiritual folk—when they have done something praiseworthy—will say (to reroute thanks), "Just give thanks to God." Paul does give thanks *to* God (in 1:3-5), but he is not shy about turning the spotlight on humans who ought to be praised.

Exercise: In the space below write a memo of thanks to God for the qualities in someone you know.

God, thank You for these qualities in _____ :

In Colossians 1:5 we meet the classic Biblical trio of faith, hope, and love. Amy Carmichael penned:

> Give me the *love* that leads the way;
> The *faith* that nothing can dismay;
> The *hope* no disappointments tire;
> The passion that will burn like fire.
> Let me not sink to be a clod.
> Make me Thy fuel, flame of God.

Note the same trio (faith, hope, and love) in Romans 5:1-5; I Corinthians 13:13; Galatians 5:5, 6; I Thessalonians 1:3; 5:8; Hebrews 6:10-12; 10:22-24; and I Peter 1:3-8.

Consider how others have answered this question. For instance:

"To my mind, Carol embodies love. She was willing to befriend an alcoholic, confront her with the problem, help her find a job, and even cope with some abuse."

"Vernon Schlief reminds me of faith. He trusted God to meet some amazing financial needs. I'll never forget him saying, 'I could go out in the forest and I believe God would provide all my needs.' "

"Hope is crystallized for me in Gloria. She has simply refused to let those hulking setbacks halt her progress. In spite of her recent injury, she still looks toward the future."

 The unbeliever treats life as hopeless but not to be taken seriously. The believer treats life as serious but not hopeless.

—Rev. Paul Kopp

Life with Christ is an endless hope;
Life without Christ has a hopeless end.

—Source unknown

Paul wrote to Colossian Christians of "the hope that is stored up for you in heaven" (1:5). The "stored up" is a common business term. In ancient manuscripts it shows up on storage receipts with the idea of "stored," "kept," or "housed" in a safe place.

? Is the Christian hope just "pie in the sky bye and bye"? Does it become, as Marx said, an "opiate of the people," dulling them to present realities (e.g., slaves before the Civil War, with their spirituals focusing on heaven)?

Did Paul stretch the truth? (Compare Romans 1:8; Colossians 1:6 and 23). Had the Gospel been proclaimed literally to "every creature under heaven"?

Some take these statements as legitimate hyperbole (or literary exaggeration). Others view these verbs as prophetic pasts (i.e., the writer is so sure of the fulfillment of God's promises in the future that he writes of them as though they are *already* accomplished—which, in a sense, they *are*—if viewed from the perspective of an omnipotent, beyond-time God. See Rom 8:29, 30). Still others feel this universal feature is underscored because of the inroads that the elite and secretive cultists were making. By contrast, Paul's motto might have been, "All of the Gospel for all of Creation."

PROGRESS REPORT

Within the progress report Paul turns in, note the parallelism of a chiasm (*ch-* is pronounced like a "k") in verses 7 and 8. A *chi* in Greek is an x- form—"X." A chiasm is an a-b-b-a pattern, as diagrammed below.

In other words, the first and last lines match and the two middle lines match. (The rearrangement of sentences in the NIV obscures this.)

    a. As ye also *learned* of Epaphras
      b. our dear fellowservant . . .
      b. a faithful minister . . .
    a. Who also *declared* . . . your love . . .

In the two middle lines we learn who Epaphras (*EP-uh-fruss*) is, and in the two other lines we learn what he did (he "declared" so that they "learned"—the mark, by the way, of a first rate communicator).

Epaphras, a Colossian ("one of you," 4:12), became a believer perhaps through Paul's evangelism, which radiated out from Ephesus for several years (Acts 19:10). If Paul were writing from Rome, it would have meant a trip of over a thousand miles for Epaphras. Many portray him as a pastor in the Colossian church. Epaphras was a spiritual supervisor for the Colossian church, who took an intense interest in them.

 Have you ever had an "Epaphras" in your life (judging by his description in Col. 1:7, 8)? How would you describe your real (or ideal) Epaphras?

18

Observe that Paul doesn't pinpoint complaints, as if Epaphras had snitched on the Colossians. However, we must assume that the same one bringing the good news (1:4, 5, 8) also brought the bad news (of 2:4-23).

The danger signals carried by Epaphras triggered Paul's prayer in Colossians 1:9-14.

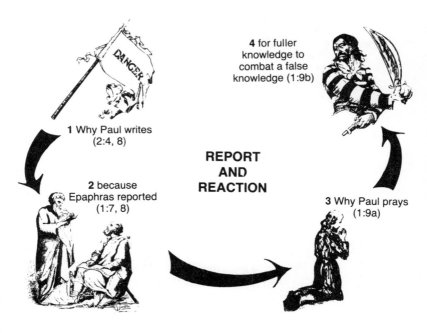

4 for fuller knowledge to combat a false knowledge (1:9b)

1 Why Paul writes (2:4, 8)

REPORT AND REACTION

2 because Epaphras reported (1:7, 8)

3 Why Paul prays (1:9a)

Next: Paul's prayer.

CHAPTER
2

TO BE A
CHRISTARCHY

Colossians 1:9-20

I often say my prayers,
    But do I ever pray?
And do the wishes of my heart
    Go with the words I say?

I may as well kneel down
    And worship gods of stone,
As offer to the living God
    A prayer of words alone.

For words without the heart
    The Lord will never hear,
Nor will He to those lips attend
    Whose prayers are not sincere.
                    —Source unknown

After Paul made his only overt reference to "the Spirit" in
Colossians, it seemed natural that such a mention should become the
launching pad for prayer. Three of the four Prison Epistles of Paul
contain somewhat similar opening prayers (Eph. 1:15-23; Phil. 1:9-11;
and Col. 1:9-14). Actually, in Colossians 1 it is not completely clear
where Paul's prayer disconnects with the following material.

Before launching into a study of Paul's prayer, we need to see what
triggered the writing of this letter. You must jump to the midsection of
the letter to discover the real reason behind Paul's writing. In
Colossians 2:4 and 8 we get the distinct signal that Paul is waving a red
flag to warn against a threatened nuisance at Colosse. A false
"philosophy" was beginning to circulate. Thus, Paul insisted on

spraying the weeds lest they choke the flowers in Colosse's spiritual garden.

To combat the insidious cult, Paul launches into one of his complicated and elaborate sentences, for which he is famed. The danger signal (undoubtedly carried to Paul by Epaphras, like a corporal reporting to his commander) triggered Paul's prayer for the Colossian church (1:9ff.). Paul partially answered his own prayer for their increased information by sending this letter.

First, Paul prays for enlightenment ("asking God to fill you with the knowledge of his will through all spiritual wisdom and understanding," 1:9). There is a cluster of key terms here: knowledge, wisdom, and understanding. "Knowledge," says Dr. William Barnhart, "is like a sharp knife. It can be used to save a life in a delicate operation or to stab a man in the heart."[1] It is significant that the implement used by both murderer and doctor is basically the same.

"Knowledge" pops up repeatedly in the first part of the Prison Epistles (Eph. 1:17; Phil 1:9; Col.1:9). It is strategic here for the precise reason that *gnosis* (KNOW-sis) or "knowledge" was just what the Gnostics (NAHS-ticks) claimed to have in a way that others didn't. Actually, the Greek word for "knowledge" has a prefix on it, giving it a flavor of fuller, clearer, or more precise knowledge.

Colossians 1:9 can be paraphrased: the "perception of God's will consists in wisdom and understanding of every sort, on the spiritual level."[2]

"Wisdom and understanding" (1:9) advance Paul's thought a step further: with knowledge, one may have only a pile of bricks. However, wisdom is the cement, and understanding is the trowel that arrange the raw material of knowledge into a usable, ordered building. In the Old-Testament the Hebrew word for "wisdom" was used of the skillful craftsmanship of Bezalel (Ex. 31:3), who was the artistic designer of Israel's portable Tabernacle. Wisdom, is "choosing the best end and the best means for reaching the end. . . . Wisdom is a matter of the mind made subservient to the will."[3] Comparing *understanding* and *wisdom* (1:9), we could say that *understanding* helps us choose between right or wrong in each case, while *wisdom* gives us the general guidelines for the decision-making *process*.

To "live a life worthy of the Lord" (1:10) courses into four power lines (four participles, or -*ing* words):

  (1) "bearing fruit" (1:10);
  (2) "growing" (1:10);
  (3) "being strengthened" (1:11);
  (4) "giving thanks" (1:12).

Paul's second prayer goal is for expanded productivity, "bearing fruit in every good work" (1:10). Fruit trees bear only one kind of fruit. In this case, however, it is helpful to visualize an imaginary tree producing oranges, peaches, apples, cherries, and all manner of mouth-watering fruit.

? Can you name an individual you have known who has manifested more than one variety of spiritual fruit (cf. Gal. 5:22, 23)? How did that fruit express itself in specific ways?

As an example, someone might say, "Larry's *kindness* came through loudly and clearly when he drove his whole family many miles to stay with Greta, his oldest daughter, who had just lost her young husband in a car accident. His first impulse as a father was to bring her right back home with them, but he exercised *patience*, or maybe even *self-control*, by counseling her to stay on in her community and face the immediate trauma of readjustment."

Just as Colossians 1:9 clusters "know" words ("knowledge," "wisdom," "understanding"), Colossians 1:11 piles up power terms ("strengthened," "power," "might"). The omniscient (all-knowing) God is also an omnipotent (all-powerful) God. The first two terms in verse 11 are actually from the same Greek root. To get this across we might render them by "empowered with power."

Paul's third request (Col. 1:11) is for enablement with power. What pictures jump into your mind when you hear the word *power*? (e.g., a body builder with rippling muscles, a jet engine revving up, a minister preaching with convicting voice tone). *Power* is an abstract word that people generally associate with concrete phenomena.

Usually we associate power with what is spectacular, sensational, supersonic, superstrong. Have you ever thought of the harnessing of heaven's power into (of all things?!?) "patience" (1:11)? People don't give trophies or hold encore applause sessions for patience. Yet God's power produces patience. And there are no instantaneous miracles of patience. Patience is as ongoing as daytime.

? Can you think of some quiet, unpublicized examples of God's power in Christians' lives?

How are "endurance and patience" in a sense counterbalanced by the word "joyfully" (in the NIV "joyfully" actually modifies "giving thanks" in vs. 12)?

On the one hand, many people associate endurance with a grim and prim poker-faced expression. By itself, endurance produces stoics. A person who has calloused hands can endure a day of chopping wood, whereas a tenderhanded city slicker cannot. Endurance, for him, would bring blisters.

On the other hand, "joyfully" brings to mind pictures of bubbling buoyancy. There is a proverbial expression that says, "he's as happy as if he had good sense."

Paul prays here that the Colossians will have a sensible joy, a joy that does more than gurgle, a joy that coexists with endurance and patience.

"endurance and patience"　　　　　　　　　　　　　　　"joyful"

Martin Luther used the illustration of a drunk trying to mount a horse and falling off the opposite side. Then, proceeding to remount, the drunk fell off the other side of the animal. Paul does not cater to either extreme. He helps balance the elements of endurance and enjoyment in the Christian.

Many scholars hold that "patience" is endurance directed toward things (i.e., adverse circumstances) whereas "longsuffering" is endurance directed toward difficult people. (Here we have used the terminology of the KJV in 1:11.)

 Given the above distinction, can you think of actual situations where you exercised "patience" and "longsuffering" as just defined? Is there a time for a Christian to stop being "longsuffering" and confront the problem person with the irritating matter? Explain.

The "we thank God" of verse 3 is matched by the "giving thanks to the Father" of verse 12. Hence, Paul shifts from his

Goals concerning the Colossians (in 1:9-11)
to
Gratitude centered in Christ (1:12-14).

Thanks is targeted toward "the Father, who has qualified you" (1:12). The threefold work of the Father is said to be that He:
1. "qualified you" (12);
2. "rescued us" (13); and
3. "brought us into the kingdom" (13).

? Can you recall a situation where you felt overly unqualified?

One uninitiated person might remember a first time he was told to hike a football and go out into the flat for a pass.

Another may recall the first time an insurance salesman waded into a swamp of technical insurance terminology for which the listener had NO previous qualifications for understanding such jargon. When feelings like that threaten to submerge our spirits, how nice it is to know that we have a Qualifier!

The imagery of the illustration in verse 12 ("to share in the inheritance of the saints") most likely comes from the Israelites' inheritance of the land. This concept is then converted into the Christian's Canaan. Christians can do more than sing (in the words of the old spiritual): "I'm bound for the Promised Land." Even now they are "a chosen people, a royal priesthood, a holy nation" (I Pet. 2:9). They "share in the inheritance of the saints in the kingdom of light" (Col. 1:12).

There are double doors in Colossians 1:13.

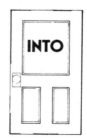

The first door shuts on the negative; the second door opens into the positive. One is the exit door ("rescued"); the other is the entrance door ("brought into").

How does archaeology help us? One thing archaeologists do is to discover ancient documents. In those secular documents are found many of the same words that are used in the Bible. Some of these words can provide illuminating illustrations of truth.

For instance, in ancient literature we find references to mass migrations or wholesale deportations of a subjugated nation by a conquering country. The Jewish historian Josephus[4] uses Paul's verb "brought us into" (Col. 1:13) when writing about how the Assyrian monarch Tiglath-pilesar "transported [Paul's verb] them [the Israelites] into his own kingdom." The same Greek verb is used to describe how Antiochus III (second century B.C.) transported several thousand Jews into Asia Minor.

 When Scripture talks about "the Kingdom of God," is it talking about something present or future? Look up the following references in order to decide.

Luke 11:20	Matthew 6:10
John 3:5	Matthew 25:31-34
Romans 14:17	I Corinthians 15:50
Colossians 1:13	II Timothy 4:1, 18

Undoubtedly you will arrive at the same conclusion from this sampling of New Testament passages that most students have: the Kingdom is *both* present (column 1) and future (column 2). Therefore, in any given context we must always ask which phase of God's Kingdom is being considered.

In God's Son we have "redemption" (1:14; cf. Eph. 1:7). Like slaves on the auction block, we have had our freedom purchased for us; we have "the forgiveness of sins" (1:14).

By gliding into Christ's work in his prayer (1:9-14), Paul has set the stage for a classic on the preincarnate Christ. Here in Colossians 1:15-20 we reach a pinnacle of New Testament Christology (the concentrated study of Christ's person).

> Fifteen men on the dead man's chest—
> Yo-ho-ho, and a bottle of rum!

Such was the crude sea song that scar-cheeked, pigtailed Cap'n Billy Bones sang at the Admiral Benbow Inn in *Treasure Island*. If music is the spillway for the human spirit, then Billy Bones's song told the tale of a pirate who died from too much rum.

But what about us, who have been rescued and redeemed (Col. 1:13)? We also have a song. Many Bible scholars believe that in

Colossians 1:15-20 Paul incorporated a hymn already being sung by the early Christians. Let's approach this by asking: How would you recognize a hymn (if a pastor quoted one in a sermon) apart from seeing its musical score? Our hymns usually have (1) rhyming lines, (2) poetical words, and (3) a definite rhythm. But Biblical poetry did not use the devise of rhyme. So then, how have scholars come to think a hymn fragment is present in these six verses?

There are certain telltale structural features that may earmark a Scriptural passage as a hymn. First, the word *who* often served as a launching pad into a hymn. Philippians 2:6-11 starts with "Who" and is printed poetically by the NIV as a hymn. Furthermore, check I Timothy 3:16 in the NIV (the "He" is "Who" in Greek):

> He appeared in a body,
> > was vindicated by the Spirit,
> was seen by angels,
> > was preached among the nations,
> was believed on in the world,
> > was taken up in glory.

Hebrews 1:3ff. may be yet another example, for in Greek it also begins with "Who." Likewise, Colossians 1:15 starts with "Who" in Greek, as it does in the KJV. One characteristic, then of possible early Christian hymns is the opening word, "Who."

By comparing these same four passages, we discover that all four have a second feature in common—they all contain lofty presentations in praise of the person and work of Christ. The elegant, elevated language is not our ordinary talk-style. Compare, for instance, a modern hymn, based on passages such as Colossians 1:15 and Hebrews 1:3a:

> True image of the infinite
> > Whose essence is concealed;
> Brightness of uncreated light,
> > The heart of God revealed.

The style suits the subject.

A third shared feature is the tendency to use elegant language, characterized by rarer Greek words. For instance, in Hebrews 1:3, 4 the Greek words for "radiance," and "exact representation," as well as the particular phrase "in heaven," are found only at this spot in the New Testament. Likewise, in Colossians 1:15-20 both "supremacy" (1:18) and "making peace" (1:20) occur only here in the Greek New Testament. Also, the Greek word for "reconcile" in Colossians 1:20 is found again only in 1:22 and Ephesians 2:16. This argues then that

Paul was picking up vocabulary that he did not ordinarily use.

The fourth feature on these four selected passages is that they all demonstrate parallelism. Parallelism means that statements function something like the two irons of a railroad track. Statement two reinforces or parallels statement one.

While the arrangement of these verses into groupings or strophes is a matter of opinion, one possible arrangement below highlights a number of the parallel features.

The Hymn in Colossians 1:15-20

Who is (the) image of the invisible God,
    Firstborn of all creation,
    <u>Because in him</u> were created **all** things
        in heaven and upon earth—
        visible and invisible,
        whether thrones or dominions
        or rules or authorities;
    all things <u>through Him</u> and for Him stand created
And He is before **all** things,
    and **all** things in Him cohere
And He is the head of the body—
    the church.

Who is (the) Beginning,
    Firstborn of the dead,
        in order that in **all** things He might become preeminent,
    <u>because in Him</u> (the Father) willed
      all the fullness to reside,
    and <u>through Him</u> to reconcile **all** things unto Him
        whether things upon earth
        or things in heaven
    making peace through the blood of this cross
    <u>through Him</u>.

 What parallel features do you spot in this arrangement of the hymn?

Did you spot the following parallels?
1. "Who is" in 1:15 matches "Who is" in 1:18;
2. "Firstborn of all creation" (1:15) parallels "Firstborn of the dead" (1:18);
3. "Because in Him" (1:16) is echoed in 1:19;
4. "And He is" appears twice in 1:17, 18.

27

One last argument that this is an early hymn (as it were, scissored out of a hymnal and pasted onto his letter by Paul in order to make his point) is the "observable shift" from personal pronouns ("you," "us," and "we" in vss. 12-14). There are none of these personal pronouns in verses 15-20 until we come to verse 21, where immediately the "you" is resumed.

One phrase couched in the midsection of the hymn, which has been puzzling to some, is the title in the KJV "firstborn of every creature" (1:15). When it is translated that way, it sounds like Christ is a creature. This subject will be treated in detail in chapter 10.

The Jewish book *Wisdom of Solomon* (1:14) stated, "For he created all things that they might exist." This is affirmed of Christ in Colossians 1:16. This umbrella statement includes:

> *The poinsetta plants in Bermuda lanes and the blue Gentian on*
> *Alpine paths, the deep brown eyes of a human friend, and the*
> *transparent green wings of a grasshopper. The gnarled Cypress of the*
> *California coast, and the orderly palms of Montreuxs quay, the . . .*
> *individual snowflakes . . . .*
>
> —Edith Schaeffer, Hidden Art

Indeed, "all things bright and beautiful" were created by Christ (Col. 1:16). Not only was all created by Christ (1:16), but all coheres (or "hold[s] together," 1:17) in Christ. Christ is, as it were, the cosmic cement. He is God's glue for our globe.

Up till now, man derived his coherence from his Creator. But from the moment that he consecrates his rupture with him, he finds himself delivered over to the passing days, and to wasted sensibility.
> —Albert Camus, existentialist philosopher

Atoms by themselves would be like a heap of loose nails which need to be magnetized if they are to hold together.
> —Augustus Strong, *Systematic Theology*

Human beings are distributed all around the earth and stand with their feet pointing towards each other . . . and . . . earth itself hangs suspended and does not fall and carry us with it.
> —Roman historian Pliny

According to Hebrews 1:3 Christ holds everything up; according to Colossians 1:17 Christ holds everything together. When everything seems to be coming unglued, we can seek Christ at the core of things.

Can you give a real-life illustration of how Christ brings meaning or coherence to one's life?

Not only is Christ "the firstborn over all creation" (1:15), but also He is "the firstborn from among the dead" (1:18); that is, He is over His new creation—the Church. (The truth of Christ's Church will be treated more in chapter 10.) Christ is also "the head of the body, the church" (1:18).

The expression "that . . . he might have the supremacy" is found only in Colossians 1:18 in the Greek New Testament. A. T. Robertson rendered it "that he himself . . . may come to hold first place."[5]

Christ should have first place in our hearts because He holds first place in the Father's heart (1:19). Why don't you give Him first place in your heart? If Christ is over all, is He over me? **Am I a walking Christarchy?**

Christ's reconciling work (1:20) will be discussed at greater length in chapter 9 of this book. Christ is able "to reconcile . . . all things" because of His cross work in "making peace through his blood, shed on the cross" (1:20). At rock bottom of it all, Christ "himself is our peace" (Eph. 2:14).

Vernon Grounds told a story from the U.S. Civil War. The war had been officially ended. Yet one day a soldier, wearing a dirty, tattered Confederate uniform, leaped out of a thicket in West Virginia and grabbed the bridle of a Union soldier's horse, "I don't want to hurt you, but give me bread. I'm starving." The man on horseback replied, "Then, why don't you go to the town and get food?" "They'll shoot me" was the answer.

The soldier had been a deserter and was under the impression that if he returned to his own troops, he would be shot. He had lived on roots and berries in the woods until his starvation was driving him mad.

The man on horseback had good news for the deserter. "Don't you know the war is over? Lincoln has pardoned the whole Confederate Army. You can have all the food you want." And with that the horseman pulled a newspaper clipping out as documented proof of General Lee's surrender.

That Southern soldier was unaware that amnesty had been declared, that peace was made, that he need not starve. Still, he needed someone to "preach . . . peace" (Eph. 2:17) to him, informing him that peace had been made (Eph. 2:15; Col. 1:20). Are we acting as God's Peace Corps, informing spiritually starving humanity that God is offering them the terms of peace if they'll only lay down their arms?

> Oh the peace forever flowing
>   From God's thoughts of His own Son;
> Oh the peace of simply knowing
>   On the cross that all was done.

CHAPTER
3

I'VE GOT A SECRET
Colossians 1:21—2:7

Colossians 1:15-20 is one of the all-time classics on the person and work of Christ. In the body of the hymn about Christ we learn that Christ came to "reconcile . . . all things" (1:20). And if Christ came to "reconcile . . . all things" (1:20), then it logically follows that "you" are included in what "he has reconciled" (1:22).

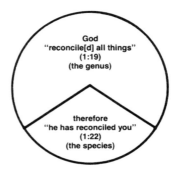

One implication of the word *reconcile* is that something is out of order and needs righting. Colossians 1:21, 22 represents this changeover in terms of a before-and-after pose ("Once," vs. 21; "But now," vs. 22).

In Colossians 1:21 and 22 the "before" and "after" are signaled by the words "alienated" and "reconciled." Inside the term "alienated" we can spot the base word "alien." In an age of space thrillers (like *Star Wars* and *Star Trek*) a visual image may form in our minds upon hearing the word "alien." We may imagine a green, scale-faced, large-and-pointed-eared, nonhuman creature from another planet. Or one might immediately associate the term with the phrase "illegal alien" (i.e., someone from another country who hasn't gone through the legal process of entry). Like the word "foreigner," the term "alien" is often used in an unkind way. The alien, picking up on the indirect vibrations or direct cutting comments, senses the "you-don't-belong-here" atmosphere. An alien wants belongingness. An alien hungers for someone to say, "You can feel right at home here."

Apart from Christ, all of us are aliens—"alienated from God" (1:21). We were "once continuously and persistently out of harmony with God."[1] The alienation is manufactured on our side and not from God's.

Once Christians were "enemies" toward God (Rom. 5:10). Like soldiers with rifles behind barricades in the French Revolution, we had declared our declaration of independence from God. Such people are "hostile in disposition as shown by . . . wrongdoings," translates Charles B. Williams (1:21).

The means of being reconciled to God is "by Christ's physical body through death" (1:22; cp. Rom. 8:3). The purpose of Christ's reconciling death was "to present you holy in his sight, without blemish and free from accusation" (1:22).

 The Greek verb for "present" was "often employed in legal language [of that time outside the Bible] with the meaning 'to bring another before the court' "[2] The same verb is used in II Corinthians 4:14; 11:2; and Ephesians 5:27 of the Christians future presentation to Christ at His coming again.

Just as a sacrificial lamb might receive the Good Priestkeeper's Seal of Approval, even so the Christian should be "without blemish" upon inspection (1:22). Paul expended his energies in that effort (1:29).

The goal would be gained, Paul penned, "if you continue in your faith." We might render the "if" by "assuming" or "provided that."

 The sure proof of election is that one holds out to the end.
—Jonathan Edwards

If it is true that the saints *will* persevere to the end, then it is equally true that the saints *must* persevere to the end.
—P. T. O'Brien

Colossians 1:23 focuses upon the human perseverance (as do I Cor. 15:2 and Heb. 3:6) rather than upon the heavenly preservation (as do Phil. 1:6 and Jude 24). This Christian continuance means being "established and firm, not moved from the hope held out in the gospel" (1:23).

How would you rate yourself on stability? How do you think others would rate you? What do you think are some character traits of the unstable person?

In Colossians 1:23 Paul piles up a threefold description of stability. "Established" or "settled" (KJV) may picture the stability of a house on bedrock (Mt. 7:25), or a person who is seated. The expression "not moved away" is found only here in New Testament Greek. We speak of unstable people as "shifty." "They must not be like a house in a region of earthquakes that is constantly shaken or on a sandy foundation and constantly changing"[3] Are you a San Andreas Christian?

"The hope . . . in the gospel" (1:23) is the hope *derived from* the gospel. The Gospel is the source and breeding ground for hope. This Gospel was once called by Paul "my gospel" (Rom. 2:16). What is Paul's role in the Gospel of reconciliation? Colossians 1:23ff. answers that question. Paul has been given "the ministry of reconciliation" (II Cor. 5:18).

A Perplexing Problem

"This . . . gospel . . . has been proclaimed to every creature under heaven" (1:23). Really, Paul? How so? One scholar, Ernst Kasemann, claims such statements are the "dream of a man who tried to do in a decade what 2000 years have not managed to do." Was Paul's evangelistic license getting the best of him? Did Paul's figures—like the attendance figures of some modern evangelists—outstrip the facts? See the comments on Colossians 1:6. One solution lies in the New English Bible's more acceptable translation "in the whole creation [rather than 'to every creature'] under heaven" (Mk. 16:15). In another sense, in Romans 10:16-18, Paul envisioned the earth as evangelized by nature, as he quoted Psalm 19:4 to prove his point.

A Second Perplexing Problem

How can Paul say that by his sufferings he "fill[s] up . . . what is still lacking in regard to Christ's afflictions"? Does he mean that there was something insufficient in the saving sacrifice of Christ upon the Cross of Calvary?

The answer to the last question must be emphatically: No! The Book of Hebrews is almost redundant with the assertion that the saving sacrifice of Christ is a once-for-all, permanent and perfect offering for sin (see Heb. 9:12-14, 25-28; 10:1-4, 9-12, 17, 18). There is no way that humans by their own meritorious suffering can "have a treasure of works laid up with the Most High" to contribute to their own salvation, as II Esdras 7:77 (Apocrypha) teaches. "A Simon of Cyrene may bear the cross, but only Jesus of Nazareth may bear the sin."[5]

The question of its meaning is further complicated by the fact that the Greek verb for "fill up" is found only here in the New Testament, and this particular Greek expression for "Christ's afflictions" is never joined together elsewhere in the New Testament in referring to the sufferings of Jesus upon the Cross.

Perhaps the best explanation of the meaning of Colossians 1:24 is to be found in the Hebrew concept of corporate personality. Let's illustrate first with that corporate idea from the suffering servant in Isaiah. Isaiah contains a series of passages about "my [God's] servant," commonly called the Servant Songs of Isaiah (42:1-4; 49:1-6; 50:4-9; 52:13—53:12). Who is the "servant" in

Isaiah 41:8?
Isaiah 44:21?
Isaiah 48:20?
Isaiah 49:3?

Answer: Obviously, it is Israel. However, does Israel exhaust the meaning of God's mysterious servant in Isaiah? From passages such as Isaiah 49:6 the answer would seem to be "no." In Isaiah 49:6 the servant's job role is "to restore . . . Israel." How could Israel restore Israel? We would have an unsolvable riddle. However, the answer lies in the Hebrew idea of corporate personality. In the servant concept we are not dealing with a simple and single personality, but a complex concept that covers more than one character.

From passages such as Matthew 8:17, Mark 15:28, and preeminently Acts 8:30-35, Christians can identify the Suffering Servant of Isaiah 53 as Jesus. Interestingly, the apostles quoted Isaiah 49:6 in Acts 13:47, thereby indicating that they saw themselves as an extension of Isaiah's servant, or an extension of the servant role. Study the diagram below with F. F. Bruce's quote—to see how the servant takes on the character of a corporate or complex personality. The servant is Israel, is Christ, is the apostolic messengers, etc.

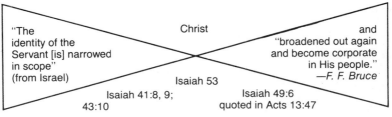

"The identity of the Servant [is] narrowed in scope" (from Israel)

Christ

and "broadened out again and become corporate in His people."
—F. F. Bruce

Isaiah 53

Isaiah 41:8, 9; 43:10

Isaiah 49:6 quoted in Acts 13:47

If the servant idea can be understood in terms of a corporate (or multiple) personality (i.e., Israel, Messiah, apostles), so also there is no reason why the suffering servant idea may not also be complex. In Colossians 1:23 Paul called himself a "servant" before he spoke of filling up Messiah's sufferings. Just as the servant's role of enlightening the Gentiles is carried on by the apostles in Acts 13:47, even so the servant's suffering role is adopted by Paul in Colossians 1:24. Like his master, Paul was a suffering servant. In fact, part of Paul's commission at conversion entailed future suffering (Acts 9:16). Just as when the unbelieving Saul had persecuted Christians—and so been persecuting Christ (Acts 9:4), so when Paul was being persecuted, he was mysteriouly identified with the suffering servant. This is one very reasonable understanding of the problem presented by Colossians 1:24.

It is now Paul's "turn" at the bat, to use a baseball figure.
                    —A. T. Robertson, *Word Pictures in the New Testament,* IV

   The dragonfly rends his husk and harnesses himself in a clean plate of sapphire mail for a pilgrimage to the dewy fields lasting but a few days; yet no flowers on earth have a richer blue than the color of his cuirass. So in the spiritual sphere, the richest garments of the soul are spun on the looms of prayer and dyed with the travail that fills up the sufferings of Christ.

                    —Leonard Ravenhill, *Why Revival Tarries*

    So send I you to labor unrewarded,
         To serve unpaid, unloved, unsought, unknown,
    To bear rebuke, to suffer scorn and scoffing;
         So send I you to toil for me alone.
    So send I you to hearts made hard by hatred,
         To eyes made blind because they will not see,
    To spend, though it be blood, to spend and spare not,
         So send I you to taste of Calvary.
                    —Margaret Clarkson

Paul Christens Suffering

Not only did Paul suffer in relation to the mystery (1:24), but he was entrusted with the privilege of speaking about it in Colossians 1:25ff. The King James Version says that Paul was given a "dispensation" (1:25). Like being handed the responsibility of overseeing a large estate, Paul had an administrative assignment, or "commission."

   Colossians 1:26 indicates that this "mystery" was a sort of temporarily padlocked secret. During Paul's day there were "mystery" religions, i.e., religious societies that maximized their own secret approaches by revealing them only to the initiated. The marrow of the mystery is implied in Colossians 1:27. Paul's mystery seems to have two main ingredients: that God has opened His treasure chest "among the Gentiles" (Col. 1:27), establishing them on equal footing with Jews in the Church (Eph. 2:14-19); and that the Messiah would actually reside "in you" (1:27). While it is a tremendous truth that Christ lives inside a believer ("in you"), it must be observed that the preposition "in" used with a plural pronoun "you," as here, may mean "among you" as a group. That this is the probable meaning is shown by the parallelism in 1:27:

> "among the Gentiles"
> "in you"
> ("among" and "in" are the same Greek preposition)

? What do you think of the spiritual slogan, "Stop trying and start trusting"? Does struggle in Christian experience show a lack of victory?

HUMAN EFFORT	DIVINE EMPOWERMENT
I labor (1:29)	
struggling (1:29)	with all his energy (1:29)
	which so powerfully works (1:29)
I am struggling (2:1)	

? Do you think you might wrongly overemphasize one side of the diagram as over against the other side's content?

Colossians 1:29 and 2:1 could help the following individual cases. Jeanette is a person of virtually hyperactive temperament. Almost every night she is in a church program or social work. She expresses considerable frustration with a pressurized schedule. But you are more concerned with the way she constantly frets over, or verbally insults, the people she is supposedly helping through her activities! As a result, you have begun to wonder what her true motivation is in all this frenzied action.

By contrast, Steve is rather laid back. He uses a lot of spiritual-sounding clichés. However when approached by a deacon who asks him to help out in a Sunday school class or, several months later, to go visit new church contacts with another Christian, Steve replied, "I'm waiting on the Lord's leading."

How do Colossians 1:29 and 2:1 help level the seesaw of positions adopted by Jeanette and Steve? (In Jeanette's case, she would do well to discover if it is really God who is energizing her projects. She may need to meditate on Martin Luther's "Did we in our own strength confide, our striving would be losing." In Steve's case, he is using clichés as a cop-out. God is providing him *inspiration*—through opportunities offered—but Steve doesn't want to put out any *perspiration* to get involved.)

In light of Colossians 1:29 and 2:1, is struggling normal or subnormal for the Christian? While every day may not require us to struggle, Paul does not represent struggle as an abnormality. In fact, his "struggling" is in perfect harmony with God's energizing. Thus, to be wrestling with someone's problem or going through emotional upheaval is not automatically subpar Christian experience. Spiritual struggle initiates us into a guild of strugglers, among whom is Paul (see also II Cor. 1:8). Indeed, "struggling" in 1:29 represents the Greek word from which we derive our word "agonize."

Unearthed Treasures

Out of Paul's struggle emerges a statement of purpose in Colossians 2:2, 3. It resembles a three-stage rocket.

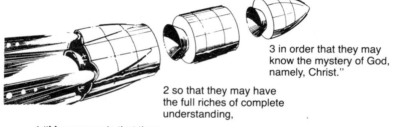

3 in order that they may know the mystery of God, namely, Christ."

2 so that they may have the full riches of complete understanding,

1 "My purpose is that they may be encouraged in heart and united in love,

 In Robert Louis Stevenson's *Treasure Island* pirate rogues sent Black Dog and Blind Pew to give Cap'n Billy Bones the "black spot" (for you landlubbers, the "black spot" is a charred spot on a piece of paper, serving as a death notice to the receiver). "It's my old sea chest they're after," Bones tells Jim Hawkins in the Admiral Benbow Inn.

Later, the dead captain's sea chest is found to contain a brace of pistols, a tin cannikin, a Spanish watch, and an oilcloth packet with guineas and other coins. But the most significant item is the discovery of Captain Flint's treasure map. There, amid scratchings of latitude and longitude in Cap'n Bones's tottering handwriting, is the drawing of an island with the words "Bulk of treasure here."

Colossians also deals with top secrets ("the mystery," 1:26) and buried treasure. In Christ "are hidden all the treaures of wisdom and knowledge" (2:3).

Interestingly, the Greek for "treasures" is the word from which we derive the English word *thesaurus*. In Stevenson's *Treasure Island* the 700,000 British pounds of gold was missing when the pirates located the treasure chest. But Colossians makes available to all "the glorious riches of this mystery, which is Christ in you" (Col. 1:27).

 Can you recall some incident where the stupendous treasure of the "surpassing greatness of knowing Christ Jesus" (Phil. 3:8) came through with impact upon you?

You might recall, for instance, being overcome with emotion upon hearing a powerful rendition of Handel's *Messiah*. Another person might reflect upon the derivative *thesaurus*, and comment that, just as a thesaurus reveals the multiple nuances of a word, Christ is multifaceted in all His attributes and titles.

At any rate, where there is treasure to be gained, expect to find pirates nearby. Thus, after Paul raises the "treasures" (Col. 2:3) for the first time in Colossians, he hints clearly that there is a threat hovering near the treasure (Col. 2:4). There are philosophical pirates nearby who want to plunder peoples' spiritual treasure. To counterattack this threat, Paul the sea captain issues an "all hands on deck" command.

By changing the metaphor slightly, we might view Paul as an army Colonel looking over the battlelines of his fighting men. This picture is based on the meaning of the Greek words for "how orderly you are and how firm" in the verse. The words "orderly" and "firm" are used in secular Greek situations of soldiers standing in straight formation and presenting a solid front against enemy forces. The Greeks were famous for a battle formation called the *phalanx* (FAY-lanx), which proved effective in their war efforts. The ancient Greek writer Xenophon (ZEN-uh-fuhn) around 400 B.C. spoke of being "filled with admiration at beholding the . . . order [same Greek word as in Col. 2:5] of the [Greek] army."[6]

 In the Colossian controversy Paul is complimenting the Christians for presenting a united front against foes of their faith. Can you think of a time when a Christian consensus made a decided difference?

One might recall a time when an adult Sunday School class was visited by two newcomers. As that Sunday's discussion progressed, it became evident that the newcomers wanted to import unorthodox ideas into the church. However, the class was entrenched in the Christian faith, and, without being obnoxious, wouldn't hedge. As a result, they were never visited by the persistent pair again. When the battle lines became drawn, the Christian soldiers stood their ground and exhibited a united front.

In Colossians 1:23 Paul urged his Colossian readers to "continue in your faith, established and firm . . . " At that point he then digressed for a bit about his own role (Col. 1:23b—2:4) until he has now come back to the subject of the Colossians' firmness in their faith (Col. 2:5). Hence, Paul refers again to being "strengthened in the faith" (2:7). By "faith" here he probably means not the active, inner process of *believing* or trusting (such as in Mt. 17:20), but that objective body of *beliefs*—being threatened by the cultists at Colosse.

Paul's statement in 2:6 is apt to be misunderstood. Many understand "just as you received Christ" to mean: In the same manner as you received Christ (i.e., by faith), now live in that manner—by faith. In other words, the whole Christian life is a faith life. While Romans 1:17 specifies the unquestioned truth that Christianity "is by faith from first to last," Colossians 2:6 probably means otherwise. The Greek word "received" is often a technical term for the passing along of traditional teaching (I Cor. 11:23; 15:1; I Thess. 2:13; II Thess. 3:6). Therefore, Paul appears to urge the Colossians to clench tightly "the pattern of sound teaching" they heard from him (II Tim. 1:13; cf. Rom. 6:17). He is thereby putting his imprimatur upon the correct concept of Christ they had received through Epaphras.

In order to immununize ourselves against doctrinal infection, Paul outlines four ways to walk in Colossians 2:7—

1. "rooted" like a tree; next he moves from an agricultural analogy to an architectural one—
2. rising like a tower, i.e., "built up in him";
3. reinforced in true teaching—"strengthened in the faith as you were taught"; and
4. running over with thanksgiving, or "overflowing with thankfulness."

Ralph Martin called Paul's pictures a "pardonable mixture of metaphors" (*Colossians and Philemon*, p. 78).

 What modern pictures might be used for solidness and stability? What ingredients make a Christian congealed against error?

Just as Paul opened (1:3) and closed (1:12-14) one section of Colossians on the note of thankfulness, once more he makes a seam with the needle of thankfulness (2:6, 7).

CHAPTER
4

PHILOSOPHICAL PIRATES

Colossians 2:8-23

Buried treasure attracts pirates like honey attracts flies. Consequently, in Colossians 2:8 Paul fires a cannon blast against the philosophical pirates of the Colossian cult. While Colossians 2:16-23 provides the closest thing to a layout of the cultists' creed, their jargon words and pet phrases are sprinkled throughout the letter. By digging beneath Paul's warnings we gather that they promoted a "philosophy" (2:8) based on a secret "mystery" (1:26, 27) and hidden "knowledge" (1:9). Their secretiveness gave them an aura of "wisdom" (1:9, 28; 2:23). Undoubtedly they proclaimed that they were getting initiated into the "fullness" of the deity (1:19; 2:9), implying that the Christians possessed something less than they did.

Notice the parallelism of Colossians 2:4 and 8:

Col. 2:4—"that no one may deceive you
by fine-sounding arguments"

and

Col. 2:8—"that no one takes you captive
through . . . deceptive philosophy."

Thus, the spiritual air-raid siren is sounded in these two verses. Beware of Biblical buccaneers with the Jolly Roger flying on the horizon. Up until Colossians 2:4 and 8 there have only been veiled hints of any serious problems posed by these "pirates," but at this point Commander Paul mans the guns.

What the behind-the-scene cultists at Colosse were promoting most probably they called a "philosophy," but Paul called it "hollow and deceptive" (2:8). Ultimately, it was a fool-osophy.

Does Colossians 2:8 mean that Christians should stay away from philosophy courses at college? Most unlikely. Surely Paul is not against philosophy per se.

The New English Bible gives the word the sense of "speculations," and J. B. Phillips uses "intellectualism" to capture the drift of it. In other words, it is a much broader term than the study of Plato, Aristotle, Kant, etc. (that is, the traditional college curriculum version of philosophy). James Moffatt's translation even corralled the religious flavor of the term by speaking of "a *theosophy* which is specious make-believe."

The fact is that everyone—construction worker or executive—has a philosophy, an organized way of thinking about things and looking at the world. That is what led the ancient Greek Aristotle (about 350 B.C.) to say: "Whether we will philosophize, or whether we will not philosophize, we must philosophize." The Jewish historian Josephus referred to the brands of Jewish thinking, such as Pharisees, Sadducees, etc., as "philosophies" (the same Greek word, which is found only here in the New Testament). Any kind of specialized subject that sucks people in and seduces them from truth that is in Christ would fall under the rubric of what Paul called here "philosophy."

 Can you name some specific modern examples of religious views or secretive subjects that might be classified under the "philosophy" condemned in Colossians 2:8?

 Not only is the Greek word for "philosophy" found alone in the New Testament at Colossians 2:8, but also the same is true for the verb "takes you captive." It is composed of two Greek root forms—*sule (SUE-lay)*, meaning "booty" plus *ago (AH-go)*, meaning "to carry." Consequently, it came to mean "to carry [someone or something] off as booty."

In Greek literature outside the New Testament the same word is found in the writer:

(1) Heliodorus, for carrying off a priest's daughter;
(2) Aristaenetus, for plundering someone's house;
(3) Nicetas, for seducing a girl.

In Colossians, then, we are dealing with spiritual seducers, philosophical plunderers, would-be religious kidnappers.

 I have more respect for the burglar who puts a jimmy under my window and steals my wife's wedding ring than I have for any Ph.D. college professor who, wielding the piratical cutlass of criticism against the Bible, breaks into the house of faith.
—R.G. Lee, quoted by E. Schuyler English in *Robert G. Lee*

Christ is the yardstick by which to measure philosophy and all phases of human knowledge.

—A. T. Robertson, *Word Pictures in the New Testament, IV*

Paul's language gets to be a bit like a labyrinth. He alerts against:

> "hollow
>   and   philosophy
> deceptive

> which depends on
>   human tradition
>   and
>   the basic principles of this world"

Since Colossians 2:9 is one of the key verses on the person of Christ, it will be treated in more detail in chapter 10 of this book.

Notice in the chart below that there are a number of parallel or repeated items from chapter one of Colossians.

COLOSSIANS 1	COLOSSIANS 2
Christ is "over all . . . whether thrones or powers or authorities" (1:15, 16)	"Christ . . . is . . . the head over every power and authority" (2:10)
takeoff on Israelites entering Promised Land—"share in the inheritance" (1:12)	takeoff on Israel's circumcision rite (2:11, 12)
"we have . . . the forgiveness of sins" (1:14)	"He forgave us all our sins" (2:13)
"over all . . . powers . . . or authorities" (1:15, 16)	Christ "disarmed the powers and authorities" (2:15)
"He is the image of the invisible God" (1:15)	"in Christ [is] all the fullness of the Deity" (2:9)

If you are looking for a key verse or verses in Colossians, verses 9 and 10 of chapter 2 certainly specify something very strategic to the book:

> "**in Christ** [is] all the FULLNESS of the Deity . . . ,
>   and
> "you have been given FULLNESS **in Christ** . . . ."

41

Colossians 2:9, 10 tell us that Christians are complete in Christ. Colossians 2:11, 12 tell us that Christians are "circumcised [spiritually speaking] . . . by Christ." Verses 11 and 12 inform us how verses 9 and 10 are possible.

Time Out for Snapshots

Colossians 2:1-15 is like a pictorial fruitcake, loaded with cherries, nuts, etc. Some of the word pictures are: "treasures" (vs. 3), "orderly . . . and . . . firm" (used of orderly troops, vs. 5), "rooted" (vs. 7), "built up" (vs. 7) "overflowing" (vs. 7), "takes you captive" (used of kidnapping and looting, vs. 8), "canceled the written code" (vs. 14), and "having disarmed the powers and authorities, he made a public spectacle of them, triumphing over them" (vs. 15).

PICTURES IN COLOSSIANS 2:8-15

Christ's cross as
surgical scalpel

Christ cancels our IOU

Christ leading triumphal
procession

Joshua 5:2-9 is the story of what happened essentially at the outset of the Israelites' entrance into the Promised Land. After their supernatural deliverance, or salvation (in Exodus 12—15), God's people received a covenant sign—a badge of courage, if you will. For those Old Testament people "circumcision [was] a seal of the righteousness . . . by faith" (Rom. 4:11). "Joshua made flint knives and circumcised the Israelites" (Josh. 5:3). This is the backdrop for Colossians 2:11 and 12.

Colossians 2:11 contrasts with Old Testament circumcision. No fraction of flesh is removed when Christ performs spiritual surgery on us. Rather, our Joshua (*Jesus* is the Greek word for the Hebrew name *Joshua*) wielded His scalpel on us for "the putting off of the sinful nature" (Col. 2:11). Thus, Christ wants us not merely to deal with externals (like the cultists did; 2:20-23) but to "put to death" internal faults (3:5).

Just as circumcision was the Old Covenant sign for Jews (Col. 2:11), so baptism is a covenant symbol for Christians (Col. 2:12). Christian baptism replaces Jewish circumcision. Here is Paul's way of writing over this rite as an essential religious symbol: **Discontinued.** Thus, we experience a "circumcision of the heart" (Rom. 2:29). In another place Paul declared that "we . . . are the circumcision . . . who worship by the Spirit of God" (Phil. 3:3).

Just as Romans 6:4 speaks of being "buried with him [Christ] through baptism," so also Colossians 2:12 speaks of "having been buried with him [Christ] in baptism."

Colossians lays great stress on the believer's co-participation in Christ's risen life. Note the togetherness ("with") in these verses:

> "buried with him" (2:12);
> "raised with him" (2:12);
> "made alive with Christ" (2:13).

In Colossians 2:14 and 15 there is a parallel structure in the Greek verbs that is hidden to the English reader. It is diagrammed below.

PARTICIPLE	MAIN VERB	PARTICIPLE
"hav*ing* canceled" (2:14)	"he took it away" (2:14)	"nail*ing*" (2:14)
"hav*ing* disarmed" (2:15)	"he made a . . . spectacle" (2:15)	"triumph*ing*" (2:15)

The Greek reader can see the symmetry because the two verbs in the middle column end in *-en* and the two participles in the last column end in *-sas*, so that they sort of rhyme.

In all six of the phrases in the above chart there are word pictures. The King James Version renders the first picture word—"blotting out." For the Jewish New Year there was a prayer that ran:

> Our Father . . . blot out our transgressions . . . ;
> Our Father . . . erase . . . all the records of our guilt.
> —in Ralph Martin, *Colossians and Philemon*, p. 86

 God identifies Himself in Isaiah 43:25 (the Greek LXX version) as "I am the one who wipes out your transgressions." Ancient Greek writing material was as easily erased as a modern chalkboard. Many examples have been dug up where lines were scraped or rubbed off and new lines rewritten on top. Christians can sing concerning their sins: "God has blotted them out."

This eradication, or canceling, is step one. But the second verb ("took it away") indicates that Christ "not only canceled the debt . . . but also destroyed the document on which it was recorded."[1]

Before moving to the third word picture, we must add still another pictorial idea from the object of the verb ("canceled") in verse 15. William Hendriksen translated the complex phrases: "having blotted out the handwritten document that was against us, which by means of its requirements testified against us."[2] Many understand this document as a "signed 'IOU.' " A. T. Robertson wrote that "the debt of the Mosaic law upon the Jew . . . was like one's own autograph signed to a note that he could not pay" and "payday comes around for mortgages."[3] It would be like a prosecuting attorney standing in the heavenly courtroom and with his finger accusing us with an indictment of our indebtedness. But, the debt is canceled and the document is destroyed.

How is this accomplished? The third word picture in the first word group explains—"by nailing it to the cross." This verb is found only here in the New Testament, and this and John 20:25 are the only mention of crucifixion *nails* in the New Testament.

The fourth word picture begins the second line diagrammed in the Word Picture Chart. There are two possible meanings for this verb ("stripped off"—Weymouth, and "disarmed"—NIV). 1) In line with the first meaning, we should remember that Old Testament war prisoners were often stripped of clothing. It was a way to graphically symbolize their defeat.

2) "Disarmed" is the translation preferred by the NIV. This word picture would agree well with the military metaphor in the remainder of verse 15. Probably, the fifth and sixth word pictures can be combined, when Christ "made a public spectacle of them, triumphing over them by the cross." This picture is hoisted by Paul from the backdrop of a victorious Roman general returning to the world capital for a "triumphal procession" (II Cor. 2:14). Often in the triumphal processions of Rome's military heroes the conquered captives would be chained to the chariot wheels of the conquerors. Perhaps this would be comparable to a ticker tape parade in New York City for a Charles Lindbergh, or in Chicago for the winners of Super Bowl XX, the Chicago Bears football team.

In Colossians 2:15, therefore, Christ is viewed as the conquering Commander-in-Chief. The disarmed, malignant angelic "powers and authorities" would be the equivalent of the Conqueror's captives. In this case, Christ's criminal cross (where apparently He was losing) became His conquering chariot (where actually He was winning).

44

Percy Shelley ("Hellas") wrote:

> A Promethean conqueror came;
> > Like a triumphal path he trod
> The thorns of death and shame"
> —in Edwin Mim's, *The Christ of the Poets*

(Note: "Promethean" means "daring, heroic.")

Hymn writer Whitlock Gandy penned:

> By weakness and defeat
> > He won the meed and crown;
> Trod all His foes beneath His feet
> > By being trodden down.

(Note: "meed" means "reward.")

Or as L. H. Farrell put it in another hymn:

> By weakness and dying,
> > The victor was He.

The Victim was the Victor.

Our Chief Clues Concerning the Cultists

Turn ahead to the next page and look at the "cult clues" chart. This will give you insight into the sort of cult that evidently was operating behind the scenes at Colosse. Keep in mind that the heresy that scholars call Gnosticism (*NAHS-tih-siz-um*)—with a capital "G"—only came to its fully flowered form in the second century A.D.—*after* the time of the Apostles and the New Testament. However, by using known information about Gnosticism as if it were a bolt of cloth and the clues inside Colossians as if they were smaller pieces of cloth remnants, we can arrive at something of a match-up.

In other words, the "philosophy" behind the scenes at Colosse (2:8)

was evidently a lot like the cult called Gnosticism that came into vogue within the next hundred years.

CULT CLUES AT COLOSSE (2:16-23)

I. Jewishness (2:16, 17) in a Gentile Context (1:27)
"religious festival, a New Moon
. . . or a Sabbath day"

II. Worship of Angels (2:18)
"delights in . . . the worship of angels"

III. Mystical Experiences (2:18)
"taking his stand on visions"
(2:18, Charles B. Williams)

IV. Harsh Treatment of the Body (2:21, 23)
"Do not handle! Do not taste! Do not touch!"

In Colossians 2:16-23 Paul comes closest to a blow-by-blow description of the Colossian cult. If we had only verses 16 and 17, we might conclude that Paul's opponents were simply antagonistic Jews. However, even here this view runs aground, for the Levitical law prohibited certain foods, but not beverages. Nevertheless, it seems plain that Paul is addressing Gentiles (Col. 1:27) throughout the letter.

 In some ways the behind-the-scenes cult at Colosse was like the community at Qumran (brought to light by the discovery of the Dead Sea Scrolls in 1947). Those Jewish monks living at Qumran were probably Essenes *(EH-seenz)*, a group described by the Jewish historian Josephus. They believed "that the body is corruptible . . . , but that the soul is immortal and imperishable. They are stricter than all the Jews in abstaining from work on the Sabbath."[4] Furthermore, some Essenes disdained marriages (perhaps related to the "Do not handle" of Col. 2:21. The same Greek verb is used of sex in I Cor. 7:1). Josephus also said that the Essenes carefully preserved the names of angels (cf. 2:18). Finally, the Qumran community observed their own customized calendar (cf. 2:16). (However, the Qumran community was a little cloistered group down on the Dead Sea coastal region, while the Colossian cult was obviously in Asia Minor.)

Secondly, the Colossian cult appeared to be guilty of angelolatry (i.e., "the worship of angels," 2:18). Interestingly, about 300 years later, Michael the Archangel was worshiped as patron saint of the nearby city of Laodicea. Also the Synod of Laodicea (held in A.D. 363) warned Christians against praying to angels, showing that those ideas still infected that same area 300 years later than Paul's letter. Some scholars have even thought that the book of Hebrews was written to the Colossian area, since chapters 1 and 2 of that book imply that those Hebrew readers held a too-high view of angels and too-low view of Christ.

 Can you think of any modern counterparts to the "worship of angels" (2:18)?

Thirdly, the Colossian cult (whoever they were) appeared to be into the ecstatic, mystical, higher spiritual life. The ancient world was known for its mystery religions, which stressed secrets into which one was *initiated* (the Greek verb form of the noun *mystery*). Colossians 2:18 may mean that the cultists considered themselves specialists in mystical experiences. The margin of the King James Version supplies an alternate translation for the middle of verse 18: "taking his stand upon the things which he has seen," i.e., visions (note: many Greek manuscripts do not have the "not" found in the KJV text). The very same Greek verb form (translated "intruding into" in the KJV and "taking his stand" in other versions) has been found three times in the temple to the Greek god Apollo, which is about twenty miles above Ephesus. It seems to refer to the initiate of the mystery religion *entering into* the temple after his initiation. Presumably he had enjoyed special visions. The Living Bible paraphrases: "They have seen a vision, they say, and know you should [too]." Hence, Paul seems to be using some of the language the cultists used to describe their supposedly superior mystical experiences.

What modern ecstatic, exotic, or esoteric religious experiences could prove to be dangerous or off base (cp. Mt. 7:22; Acts 19:13-17; I Jn. 4:1)? Give some examples.

Fourthly, the cult at Colosse accented some form of asceticism, that is, "harsh treatment of the body" (2:23). Notice the parenthesis in the

King James Version, or quotation marks in the New International Version, at verse 21. This shows that the translators have properly understood the words as being not from Paul, as expressing his own true Christian view, but quoted by Paul as slogan words of Paul's opponents. This is essential; otherwise, the verse is misunderstood. In fact, you will sometimes hear Christians misuse it; for instance, they may quote it as a proof text against too much physical contact between teenagers on dates. Then it falls into the classic category of a text without a context becoming a pretext!

 Archaeologists have supplied us with an illuminating cross-reference to Colossians 2:21. At Qumran on the Dead Sea—where the Jewish religious community of monklike people lived—a copy of the guiding handbook for the community was found. It was called the *Manual of Discipline*. In that ascetic community's rule book were found admonitions like: "He shall not touch . . . " and "he shall not taste"—paralleling the very wording of Colossians 2:21!

Don'ts

Notice that the non-Christian opponents of Paul had their list of no-nos ("not . . . not . . . not"). Some Christian groups tie people up in "nots." They turn life into a grocery list of don'ts. As Puritan Richard Baxter put it, "As a child I was much addicted to play." Such people turn life into an unbearable "yoke" (Acts 15:10). One young nonestablishment woman of the sixties explained her friends' reaction to church legalism: "You see, the church I grew up in thought the big issues are dancing and sideburns. In five minutes they could appoint a high commission against playing solitaire. That's why the church of today ain't no big thing."[5] Colossians 2:21 finds its counterpart in the tone of the modern couplet:

> I don't smoke
> And I don't chew,
> And I don't go
> With boys that do.

 In what ways can a Christian overemphasize negatives?

By such spiritual-sounding slogans the non-Christian cult at Colosse was trying to bully believers into their higher life movement. Probably they said things to Christians like, "If you could only experience the wonderful truths we've entered into." But some people want to advocate a life higher than the one God does.

48

Evidently another trademark of the higher-life group at Colosse was their "false humility".

 Ted was a new student at seminary. Upon meeting his roommate, Ted observed that Jerry also owned a trumpet. "Do you play well?" Ted asked. "Not that great," Jerry replied. "How about you?" Jerry returned. "Oh, pretty fair," the healthy-spirited Ted said.

A little later when the trumpet tones actually sounded forth, Ted found himself embarrassed. Out of a supposed humility Jerry had stated that he wasn't all that good, but he was practically orchestra-level material, whereas Ted came up pretty shabbily compared to Jerry's abilities.

Many Christians seem to think that humility means putting themselves down, saying that they are less than they really are. If I am a semi-pro baseball player and am asked how well I play baseball, it is not humility to say, "Oh, so-so"; it is lying. Humility is having an accurate assessment of our abilities—not too high, but also not too low.

Beware of the pride of humility.

—Jerome (about A.D. 300)

Finally, the cultists were guilty of a "harsh treatment of the body" (2:23). Evaluate the cases below:

- A newspaper reported in 1981 that a woman starved to death because "God told her" to fast.
- A high school boy, formerly active in track, dropped all physical exercise because he wanted to "give his all to Christ."
- "Dating is not for me," said the young woman. "The Bible says, 'Set your minds on things above, not on earthly things.' "

These kind of remarks often come from people who do not understand the "God, who richly provides us with everything for our enjoyment" (I Tim. 6:17). As C. S. Lewis once said, "There is no good trying to be more spiritual than God."

5

A MATTER OF LIFE AND DEATH

Colossians 3:1-8

How Should We Then Live? is a book title by Francis Schaeffer. That title epitomizes quite well the two concluding chapters of Colossians. Jokingly, Dr. William White told about someone seeing a patient kicking and screaming on the way to the surgery room. When asked who the patient was, the inquirer was told: "Why that's Dr. So-and-so." In other words, when the theory had to be tested out in terms of applied reality, it didn't come off so well. How well does the chemical of Christianity change us in the test tube of everyday life?

This section of Scripture should be set in its setting. Colossians 2:20-23 details the wrong way to live—gnostic style. Colossians 3:1-4 directs to the right way to live. The gnostic approach to spirituality was governed by "rules" (2:20) and "regulations" (2:23). By contrast, for the Christian "Christ . . . is your life" (3:4). The wrong kind of religiosity focuses on a picky-picky outward code. True Christianity focuses on inward character and unselfish conduct. Colossians 3:1-4 is intended to be an attitude rightener.

? How could Colossians 3:1, 2 be very misunderstood and turned into a Christian gnosticism?

Colossians 3:1-4 gives:
- I. *Incentives (3:1, 2) to:*
    - A. Seek things above (3:1)
    - B. Set one's mind on things above (3:2)

- II. *Imperatives (3:3, 4)*
    - C. Enclosed (3:3)
    - D. Disclosed (3:4)

While we could use more Christian concentration and contemplation, it would be easy to misunderstand these verses out of context.

COLOSSIANS 3:1,2
MISINTERPRETED

You may have seen teenagers in a record store with headphones over their ears and a record on nearby. Only they can hear the sound, which is usually blasting away inside their own headset. They are virtually oblivious to the environment around them while they are shut in to a musical world all their own.

Some Christians give the impression that something like this is what the Christian life is all about. With their prayer and Bible study prominent, they are removed from the realisms around them. Some churches are almost like catatonic mental patients—sitting and staring off into oblivion. They are so heavenly that they are of little earthly good.

Some Bible verses (e.g., Col. 3:1, 2) and Christian hymns seem to support this removed-from-raw-realism life-style. For instance the hymn words of "Higher Ground" testify:

> My heart has no desire to stay
>   Where doubts arise and fears dismay;
> Tho' some may dwell where these abound,
>   My prayer, my aim, is higher ground.

And the next stanza begins: " I want to live above the world . . . ." This hymn may seem to support that Christian "catatonic" state, just as Colossians 3:1, 2 might also—if taken out of context. Such a life-style, however—a mental monasticism, or Christian ghetto complex—would be little more than a Christian gnosticism. If Colossians 3:1-4 is read apart from the context of the rest of the book, it sounds quite ethereal (as if, in 3:2, one ought to sit and look toward the sky). However, Colossians 3:1-4 leads us toward such down-to-earth matters as change of character (3:5-9), nondiscriminatory treatment of people (3:10, 11), and working relationships on the home front (3:18-21),

51

and in job situations (3:22—4:1). There's nothing to test Christian character like changing dirty diapers or on-the-job conflict.

Note that the "If" of the King James Version (in 3:1) has been acceptably translated "Since" by the New International Version. The idea is: assuming such and such is true . . . . The "then" in the NIV of 3:1 is the same Greek word rendered "therefore" in verse 5. Quite often, Paul made a transition to practical sections by means of the conclusion-drawing "therefore." (For examples, see Rom. 6:1; Gal. 5:1; Eph. 4:1; and Phil. 2:1 for the same Greek word.)

What's 'Therefore' There For?

Paul uses the "therefore" like a lever. Like an Archimedes with his lever, Paul found his own fulcrum, or point of leverage, in that idea that Christians "have been raised with Christ" (3:1). This catapaults us back to Colossians 2:12—"raised with him [Christ]."

Note, then, the two parallel commands that Paul used for leverage:
1. "Set your hearts on things above" (3:1);
2. "Set your minds on things above" (3:2).

A. T. Robertson said of Colossians 3:1, 2: "It is like the skylark that sings his glorious song as he flies upward into the skies."[1]

This arena is described as "where Christ is seated at the right hand of God" (3:1). This expression, found in some form in Acts 7:55; Romans 8:34; Ephesians 1:20; Hebrews 1:3; 8:1; 10:12, is not to be taken with strict spacial literalism.

I laughed when a friend said that Midwest Research Associates was located in California. (Obviously, literalism was out of place.) My friend caught my reaction and explained that Midwest Research Association began in Detroit, Michigan—thus accounting for the company name. Similarly, the right hand in Bible times was originally a place of high honor. F.F. Bruce remarked, "The apostles . . . no more thought of a location on a literal throne at a literal right hand of God than we do. It was the conventional representation that occasioned Luther's outburst: 'Oh, that heaven of the charlatans, with its golden chair and Christ seated at the Father's side vested in a choir cape and golden robe as the painters love to portray Him!' "[2]

Despite the fact that Paul said not to set our minds "on earthly things" (3:2), he was certainly not advocating irresponsibility toward earthly families (3:18-21), earthly jobs (3:22—4:1), or normal community involvement. Notice the parallelism in Colossians 3:3, 4 charted on the next page.

VERSE 3	VERSE 4
your life	your life
hidden *with* Christ	appear *with* Him
in God	in glory

Theologian James Denney called union "with" Christ the diamond pivot of Christian truth.[3] Note that Christians are viewed as:

buried with Christ (2:12);
raised with Christ (2:12; 3:1);
made alive with Christ (2:13);
connected with Christ (2:19);
hidden with Christ (3:3);
appearing with Christ someday (3:4).

CHRISTIANS ARE (3:3)

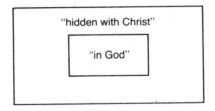

The telltale words "will" and "in glory" in verse 4 point us futureward. Here is the only place where Colossians refers to the Second Coming.

If believers aren't supposed to treat their bodies harshly (2:23), does that mean they are to unharness their physical passions? That is where Colossians 3:5ff. begins to discuss Christian standards offered in contrast to the cult standards we have just studied (in 2:16-23).

 How do you think "dead" people can "put to death" (3:5) anything?

Pirates are notorious cutthroats when treasure is around. Ordinarily pirates do not serve well as models for Christians. However, Christians, too, have a treasure (2:3). Colossians 3:5 does call upon us to unsheath our dagger for one cause—to attack our sin. In that case, we are commanded to be murderers. Imagine—Christians as killers, sin killers! Actually, verse 5 is a follow-through on two earlier "hinge" verses:

2:20—"Since you died with Christ";
3:1—"Since . . . you have been raised with Christ."

So, then, if "Christ. . . is your *life*" (3:4), you ought to "put to *death* . . . whatever belongs to your earthly nature" (3:5). As the title to this chapter suggests, Christians are engaged in a matter of life and death. It is paradoxical that, although we "died" (2:20), still we must "put to death" (3:5) specific sins. This last phrase is probably to be understood as equivalent to "count yourselves dead to sin" (Rom. 6:11).

Colossians 3:5—4:6 revolves around four catch words:
1) "Put off" (3:5-11, KJV);
2) "Put on" (3:12-17, KJV);
3) "Submit" (3:18—4:1);
4) "Pray for us" (4:2-6).

F. W. Beare claims concerning Colossians 3:5, 8, and 12: "Paul here adopts a literary form not found elsewhere in his letters; in place of a general catalogue of pagan vices such as . . . in Romans 1:26-31 and Galatians 5:19-21, he uses . . . [a scheme] of pentads [or groupings of five items]—two [lists] of vices and one of virtues."[4]

The Greek verb in Colossians 3:5 ("put to death") is found again in Romans 4:19, where it is rendered "as good as dead." Romans is speaking about Abraham's hundred year old body, which—practically speaking—was "as good as dead" as far as reproduction was concerned. Similiarly, we are to be "as good as dead" as far as sin is concerned.

"Mortify" (3:5, KJV) comes from the same root as "mortal," "mortician," "rigor mortis," etc. Christians are to be vice-vigilantes concerning their sins.

A sign over the door of a dyeing establishment read:

> I Live To Dye, I Dye To Live;
>   The More I Dye, The More I Live;
>   The More I Live, The More I Dye.

Brian Dill wrote, "Paul regards sin in much the way a fish seller regards a fish: It stinks, it's dead, and it's only good when it's off my hands."[5]

⊞ Graham Kerr, once known as TV's "Galloping Gourmet," made numerous changes after becoming a Christian. He simplified his life-style from a million dollar salary to $12,500 a year. He began investing his life in microfarms that would raise food for the world's hungry. Commenting on some of the changes, he said: "Trina [his wife] and I have not died easily. It's been blood and guts every step of the way we've had to die."[6]

The King James Version translates verse 5: "Mortify . . . your members which are upon the earth." Yet it is unlikely that Paul was referring to the actual physical "members" of the human body. Perhaps Paul was speaking in a manner similar to that of Jesus in Matthew 5:29 and 30. This is further demonstrated by the five items appearing after the colon in the NIV that show Paul was talking about specific sins. A modern approximation of this might be when we say, "I'll have none of your lip." We are not talking about physical lips in the expression, but referring to sarcastic speech that proceeds from someone's lips.

Sexual and Sinister Sins (Col. 3:5)

Below are listed the same five words and some warned-against ways in modern situations.

Sexual immorality. From this Greek word, *porneia (por-NAY-ah)*, we derive the word "pornographic." It is often translated "fornication," but is broader in coverage than premarital sex. As the NIV suggests, it includes any immoral sexual behavior. We see a modern illustration in many TV shows (soap operas) and commercials (for example, the cologne ad which says that a man should wear that cologne or "nothing at all").

Impurity. This term could be broader and more internal than "sexual immorality." It might include telling jokes that carry sexual overtones.

Lust. This could include any sinful desire, although we normally associate it with the sexual impulse. The Evangelical Press News Service letter (November 6, 1987) reported that Colonel Sanders's franchise had been named by the National Federation of Decency as one of three businesses they tagged as "Pornographer of the Month"—for using more money to advertise in pornographic magazines than any other advertisers in America. This seems incongruous in that Colonel Sanders himself was a professing Christian.

Evil desires. Like lust, this sin would extend to inner motivation. Couldn't the Christian college be guilty along the same line as the pornographer when it uses the Adonis male or knockout female for its advertisements to recruit high schoolers to its college?

Greed. Of the five sin expressions, we probably least associate greed with sexual sin. However, it may not be that far afield, for it is "the itch to get more."[7] It is "the sin of possessiveness."[8] It's the have-to-have-it habit. Babies are born with clenched fists.

 The church leader Augustine (about A.D. 300) said after his conversion, "Now was my soul free from the biting cares of canvassing and getting, and . . . scratching off the itch of lust."

William Hendriksen wrote: "These sins [of vs. 5] attract God's displeasure [of vs. 6] like a magnet attracts iron or like a high steeple on an isolated hill draws lightning."[9] (Happily, the Cross of Christ became our lightning rod!) The "wrath of God" is God's holy revulsion and recoil against unholiness, and it is consistently taught in the New Testament (Jn. 3:36; I Thess. 1:10; 5:9; Rev. 6:16).

The sins of verse 5 were once-upon-a-time, ingrained habits of these Gentile Christians, as noted by the NIV in verse 7: "You used to walk in these ways." That means, as Dennis Guernsey put it, these old grooves must be regrooved by Christ. It is as if a phonograph record needed to be regrooved. What it "used to" play was a different music. Dennis Guernsey amplified this: "Suppose you were the engineer of a long freight train travelling along a road bed at 60 miles per hour. You see something that warns you of danger ahead. You slam on the brakes, but because of the weight of the cars behind you, it's several hundred yards—even a mile—before you can stop the train. The force that carries you forward is momentum."[10]

What does Guernsey's illustration help us to learn about many new Christians?

Grasping the make-up of the early church helps to save us from a prim self-righteousness. Sinner-sinners, upon visiting a church, often get the impression from all the dress-up appearance and foreign-sounding "holy words" that there aren't any real sinners there who can empathize with their problems or feelings. But Paul named people in early congregations who were remembered to be ex-swindlers, ex-male prostitutes, former thieves, etc. ("that is what *some of you were*"; see I Cor. 6:9-11). There would be little point to Paul listing the sins of Colossians 3:5 and 8 unless there were people there who still had to fight to offset those sins in themselves. Experiential verses like Colossians 3:5 and 8 (or Eph. 4:27, 28) help counterbalance and provide a realistic understanding of doctrinal realities like II Corinthians 5:17. In other words, not every ingrained sin will necessarily be automatically and instantaneously zapped at conversion. Singer B. J. Thomas testified how God delivered him overnight from hard drugs, but when he and his wife decided to cut out smoking, it was an uphill battle.

A second pentad (or grouping of five items) is found in Colossians 3:8. Take a minute and write out an actual, modern example of each of the five sins.

1. Anger: _____

_____

_____

2. Rage: _____

_____

_____

3. Malice: _____

_____

_____

4. Slander: _____

_____

_____

5. Filthy language: _____

_____

_____

Is all anger wrong? Give Biblical support for your answer.

Psychologists might tell us that destructive anger is one emotion that can, as it were, rust and corrode our physical pipes. Anger is in itself a neutral emotion, but it is frequently used in the wrong way. Some Biblical passages that indicate that all anger or wrath is not automatically bad are Psalm 7:11; John 2:13-17; and Ephesians 4:26.

Anger. Like a latent, rumbling volcano, some Christians bury hostile feelings toward spouse or co-worker rather than honestly confronting issues.

Rage. These two Greek words are very close in meaning; perhaps there is a bit more of explosive Vesuvius in the second word. Excusing frequent temper tantrums as "getting it out of my system" might illustrate this term. A fist hole through a wicker chair also illustrates the destructive results that can remain.

Malice. This is badness in general. Turning church business sessions into verbal brawls could illustrate this quality.

Slander. Passing along juicy tidbits of gossip without even being sure of the facts is too common.

Filthy language. This refers not only to four-letter words, but also to abusive language. Somberly sharing so-and-so's sins as "prayer requests" can destroy another's self-esteem.

 Samuel Johnson said: "The difference between coarse and refined abuse is the difference between being bruised by a club and wounded by an arrow."

Irrespective of your I.Q., how's your C.Q. (character quotient) stacking up so far according to Colossians?

CHAPTER
6

A CHRISTIAN'S CHARACTER CLOTHING
Colossians 3:9-17

London was draped in fog that night. One's ears could pick up the shrill whistle of the London bobbies as they were chasing the fleeing form through the lanes of London. They cornered their quarry in the basement of a doctor's house. The man the police shot was a hideous, villainous fiend—a Mr. Hyde. But the man they buried was a kind-hearted gentleman named Dr. Jekyll. The story was crystallized in Robert Louis Stevenson's classic, *The Strange Case of Dr. Jekyll & Mr. Hyde*.

Dr. Jekyll was the physician who concocted a potion in his laboratory that would turn him into the distorted monster named Hyde. But then the time came when Dr. Jekyll no longer needed to drink the chemical in order to change into the beastly Hyde. His character changed apart from the chemical. Robert Louis Stevenson, who was a Christian, in that classic tale was grappling with one of the important ingredients in any Christian's life—that commodity called character.

While Stevenson chose to represent character through the picture of chemistry, the apostle Paul chose to represent character under the picture of clothing—character clothing.

One of the main industries at Colosse dealt with wool and weaving. Colosse was particularly noted for the reddish purple color of its cloth. Consequently, the dye color was called *Colossénos*.

It is not surprising, then, that in writing to the Colossian Christians Paul weaves into his letter the picture of clothing. Colossians 3:9-14 contains at least four such verb expressions— "taken off" in 3:9, "put on" in 3:10, "clothe yourselves" in 3:12, and "put on" in 3:14.

Also, scholars of ancient culture tell us that the mystery religions might use as many as twelve changes of clothing in their secretive initiation ceremonies. In Paul just one basic clothing change is called for—but that is more than skin deep. We may write over our old life-style wardrobe line: To be discontinued!

 Do you know any people who have a problem with shading the truth? In what area do you think you might be most likely to falsify?

 The Greek imperative in the present tense in verse 9: "You used to tell lies to one another as though it was the natural thing to do; don't do it anymore."[1] Resist the habit, whether you've ever had it or not.

The "old self" in Colossians 3:9 can be defined as "the whole personality organized for and geared in rebellion against God."[2] The former self with its raggedy practices is to be discarded.

Mental Metamorphosis

Yes, we can undergo the process of "being renewed in . . . the image of [the] Creator" (3:10). Donald Guthrie stated: "There is an implied contrast between the static practices of the old nature [as it were, stuck in a rut] and the new nature being renewed. The latter is continuous and dynamic."[3]

 What changes are there in the past several years on your spiritual progress report? Are you currently seeking change in some area?

Note that "the *new* self . . . is being *renewed*" (Col. 3:10). One of the most radical changes Christ's character clothing can bring is the way a person views those of other races, economic brackets, educational levels, etc.

 George Wallace, who had been governor of Alabama five years before being shot, told a crowd of 300, at a Baptist regional meeting, of changes that had come to him. After the assassination attempt, he had trusted Christ for forgiveness. Wallace told the racially mixed crowd that the old way of segregation and racism was wrong. Wallace said from his wheelchair that those who use the Bible to defend their racism are "dead wrong."

One group exemplifying Colossians 3:11 is First Baptist of Columbus, Mississippi. Within that congregation at one time were about a dozen Chinese students from a nearby university; two young women from India; Kezia Chogo and Patricia Getao from Nairobi, Kenya; Pam Johnson—a black native of Mississippi; Francesco Matelli—an exchange student from Italy; and a seven-year old adopted Korean child.

 What group names would you substitute in Colossians 3:11 so as to rewrite it in terms of your own world?

COLOSSIANS 3:11 CHARTED

Racial/national	"no Greek or Jew"
Religious	"circumcised or uncircumcised"
Cultural/educational	"barbarian, Scythian"
Social/economic	"slave or free"

 What does this verse have to say about the way a Christian treats a waitress, a high management executive, or a garbage collector?

 I thank God that I was born a Greek, and not a barbarian; a free man and not a slave; a man and not a woman; but above all, that I was born in the age of Socrates.

—Plato

Rabbi Judah taught that a man should say every day, "Blessed be God for not creating me a pagan, nor foolish, nor a woman."

—James Moffatt, *Introduction to the Literature of the New Testament*

Here there is no Greek or Jew, circumcised or uncircumcised, barbarian, Scythian, slave or free [and in Gal. 3:28 he added "neither . . . male nor female"], but Christ is all . . . .

—Paul the Apostle

The final four labels of people in Colossians 3:11 reveal that the early Christians were largely from the lower class. Whereas the first two pairings in the verse—Jew-Greek, circumcised-uncircumcised—are opposites, the third pair ("barbarian, Scythian") are not north and south pole to each other. Rather, Scythian is the lowest extreme on the ladder of the barbarian category.

"Barbarian" is an onomatopoeic (*ahn-uh-maht-uh-PEE-ik*) word. Onomatopoiec words, like *buzz* or *hiss* or *growl*, reproduce in their very letters something of the sound of the idea. As the *Webster's New*

Colegiate Dictionary says, the "sound suggests the sense." Probably the more refined Greeks made fun of foreigners, whose language sounded to them like *bar-bar*. To them they were *bar-bar-ians*.

Scythians first came into prominence in the seventh century B.C. At one point they were masters of Asia for twenty-eight years. The Greek historian Herodotus said, "They drank the blood of the first enemy killed in battle, and made . . . drinking bowls of the skulls of the slain."[4] What a nice bunch of guys! Later in Greek history, when the Scythians were slaves, they were portrayed as comical figures—uncouth in manner and speech.

The great Greek philosopher Aristotle had defined a slave as "a living tool, as a tool is an inanimate slave." In fact, the slave was inventoried with the other possessions of their owners, such as cattle or carts. Slaves had been put to death merely on a whimsy in some cases. Yet we must keep in mind that many slaves were prisoners of war, and so were intelligent and well-educated.

> "God so loved the world," not just the few—
> The wise, the great, the noble, and the true,
> Or those of favored class, or race, or hue.
> "God so love the world"—do you?
> —Anonymous

Christians must cut across all these human barriers, for "Christ is all, and is in all" (3:11). C. F. D. Moule understands this phrase as meaning that "Christ is all that matters" and "is 'in all' members of the [Christian] community."[5]

Earlier we saw that philosophical pirates were attacking at Colosse (2:4, 8). Those pirates betrayed their own mental wardrobe (2:16-23).

Unlike a buccaneer with his eye patch, three cornered cocked hat, gold earrings, bandanna, sailor's cape with silver buttons, and, of course, cutlass and brace of pistols, the Christian wears a very different outfit. God's catalog for the well-dressed believer includes "compassion, kindness, humility, gentleness and patience" (3:12).

Character Clothing

Now let's analyze each of the Christian character traits in greater detail. First comes "compassion." In Greek thought, this feeling was said to arise physically in the area of the viscera (the heart, lungs, liver). The same Greek word is used in its physical sense when Judas "fell headlong" and "his body burst open and all his *intestines* spilled out" (Acts 118). The popular expression "a gut-level feeling" is close to the Greek word. Compassion, then, involves being moved emotionally to relieve the need in question. The classic Biblical illustration of this is the Good Samaritan, where the sister verb to "compassion" is used in Luke 10:33.

 The famous skeptic Bertrand Russell said: "There are certain things that our age needs . . . . The root of the matter is a very simple and old fashioned thing, a thing so simple that I am almost ashamed to mention it . . . . The thing I mean—please forgive me for mentioning it—is love, Christian love or compassion."
—in Stuart Babbage, *The Vacuum of Unbelief*

 Can you think of a concrete, real-life illustration of compassion someone has shown?

Second in the character clothing to put on is "kindness." This word is used more with reference to God than to anyone else in the Greek version of the Old Testament (the apostles' Bible). Kindness is mellowed goodness.

David Livingstone, missionary to Africa, observed that big game hunters "indulged in an indiscriminate slaughter of wildlife that filled him . . . with something like disgust. Livingstone . . . called it 'butchery'."[6]

Thirdly, the homespun fabric of "humility" appears in Colossians 3:12. Humility does not mean downgrading oneself (that is "false humility," Col. 2:23), but rather having an honest appraisal of one's strengths and weaknesses; having genuine "otherishness" rather than selfishness (Phil. 2:5-8). Humility means to many people that you put yourself down. But if you are a top-notch baseball player and are asked how well you play, it is not humility to hang your head and say, "Oh, average." That is "false humility" (in fact, it's a lie).

Fourthly, "gentleness" graces the list. It is "meekness" in the King James Version, but "meekness" signifies weakness to many people. The Greek philosopher Aristotle liked to define words by what we might call the happy medium.

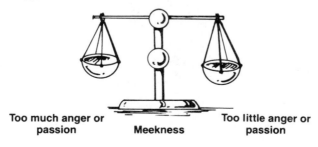

Too much anger or passion   Meekness   Too little anger or passion

The person possessed of just the right amount of self-control was the meek person. William Barclay portrays it as harnessed strength rather than spinelessness. It is like the stallion that has been broken and bridled. "Gentleness" is the large, trained dog who will play with toddlers but take on burglars.

"Patience" is the fifth item of character clothing on the rack in 3:12. Instead of being short-tempered, this means being long-tempered.

"Bear with each other" urges us to hold out at length and put up with a lot. This is a maxi-length item of character clothing.

When a debt has been cleared, a personal account squared, we are called to "forgive." Don't put this piece of character clothing in mothballs!

 David Livingstone wrote to a friend, Dr. Risdon Bennett, some twenty years after an incident: "I often think I have forgiven, as I hope to be forgiven, but the remembrance of the slander often comes boiling up, although I hate to think of it. You must remember me in your prayers that more of the spirit of Christ may be imparted to me."[7]

John Knox pinpointed the local issue of forgiveness by writing, "The whole of Colossians is more or less overshadowed by Paul's concern about Onesimus."[8]

Finally, in verse 14 is the overcoat among the character clothing, for "over all these virtues put on love."

CHARACTER CLOTHING IN COLOSSIANS 3:12-14

(God's wardrobe for the well-dressed Christian)

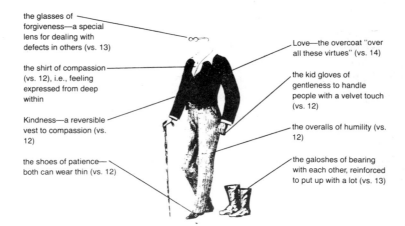

the glasses of forgiveness—a special lens for dealing with defects in others (vs. 13)

the shirt of compassion (vs. 12), i.e., feeling expressed from deep within

Kindness—a reversible vest to compassion (vs. 12)

the shoes of patience—both can wear thin (vs. 12)

Love—the overcoat "over all these virtues" (vs. 14)

the kid gloves of gentleness to handle people with a velvet touch (vs. 12)

the overalls of humility (vs. 12)

the galoshes of bearing with each other, reinforced to put up with a lot (vs. 13)

Orders to Obey

Colossians 3:15-17 climaxes with four commands:
  (1) "Let the peace of Christ rule" (15);
  (2) "Be thankful" (15);
  (3) "Let the word of Christ dwell" (16);
  (4) "Do . . . all in the name of the Lord Jesus" (17).

This section is directed to the Christian group. The plural "your hearts" in verse 15, the plural "you" and "your" in verse 16, and the "one another" in verse 16 cement this conclusion. Christianity is not a Lone Ranger religion.

The Berkeley Version renders verse 15: "Let the peace of Christ . . . be umpire in your hearts." F. B. Meyer offered a helpful illustration. On a starless night when crossing the English Channel, the ship captain pointed out a technique for moving into port. He pointed to three pinpoints of light on the shoreline. He commented, "I steer our ship until the three lights merge into one, and then I head straight into port." The believer's three guiding lights are the peace of Christ (3:15), the Word of God (3:16), and the witness of the Spirit.

? Compare Colossians 3:16 (in its context of 3:16—4:4) with Ephesians 5:18 (in its context of 5:18—6:20). Using a comparison of the parallel groupings in both contexts, what conclusion do you arrive at concerning the meaning of "be[ing] filled with the Spirit" in Ephesians 5:18?

EPHESIANS 5:18—6:20	COLOSSIANS 3:16—4:4
"Speak to one another with psalms, hymns and spiritual songs" (5:19)	"as you sing psalms, hymns and spiritual songs" (3:16)
Wives and husbands (5:22-33)	Wives and husbands (3:18, 19)
Children and parents (6:1-4)	Children and parents (3:20, 21)
Slaves and masters (6:5-9)	Slaves and masters (3:22—4:1)

If the four units of thought in the chart are essentially the same, what does that suggest about the thought that launches each of these sections? Surely it suggests that to "be filled with the Spirit" (Eph. 5:18) must vitally encompass "let[ting] the word of Christ dwell in you richly" (Col. 3:16).

If the "peace of Christ" (15) is subjective or inward, it is protectively counter balanced by the more objective "word of Christ" in Scripture (15)—although this, too, is to settle down "in you." J. B. Phillips paraphrased verse 16: "Let the full richness of Christ's teaching find its home among you." The "word of Christ" might mean the word (i.e., message, teaching) that comes from Christ or that centers in and concentrates on Christ.

 In what ways or what ideas has Christian music taught you?

In verse 16 teaching is transmitted by the mode of music. The spillway of song is channeled by the banks of teaching truth. Some have tried to formulate a threefold classification of Christian music:
1. "psalms"—The Old Testament psalter;
2. "hymns"—perhaps like the Magnificat of Mary; and
3. "spiritual songs"—spontaneous compositions.

 Once the well-known British Bible commentator Matthew Henry entered this jotting in his diary after a robbery:
  "Let me be thankful: First, because I was never robbed before; second, because although he took my purse, he did not take my life; third, although he took all I possessed, it was not much; fourth, because it was I who was robbed and not I who robbed."[9]

Colossians 3:17 is, then, a fitting climax and conclusion to this section. All of life is to be umbrellaed under the Lordship of Christ. The name of Christ is the aegis and banner under which the Christian recruit marches. In fact, if we had only one verse to sum up Christian ethics, Colossians 3:17 would be an excellent choice.

Review

Four commands climax verses 15-18. Katie Wilkinson summarized several of those commands in a hymn:

> May the peace of God my Father
>> Rule my life in everything
> That I may be calm to comfort
>> Sick and sorrowing.
> May the word of God dwell richly
>> In my heart from hour to hour,
> So that all may see, I triumph
>> Only through His power.

CHAPTER
7

HEAVEN ON EARTH
Colossians 3:18—4:6

Pirates are not renowned for being homebodies. In *Treasure Island* as the pirate Black Dog tried to con Jim Hawkins into doing his dirty work (just after swearing at him), he patted him on the shoulder and said, "I have a son of my own . . . and he's all the pride of my 'art."

The boy was not overly convinced. Neither is anyone convinced by the Christian whose homelife is a shambles. The wife who talks constantly about her husband behind his back, the husband who ignores the communication needs of his wife, the children who are rude and misbehave—all cast a shadow over their Christianity.

On a number of occasions, New Testament writers provide sweeping guidelines for family living. These tables of household instructions bear a structured similarity to each other. Besides the four passages listed on the chart below, I Timothy 2:8—6:2 provides even more elaborate exhortations on this subject, among others.

TABLES OF HOUSEHOLD INSTRUCTION

Wives and Husbands	Children and Parents	Slaves and masters
Eph. 5:22-30	Eph. 6:1-4	Ephesians 6:5-9
Col. 3:18, 19	Col. 3:20, 21	Col. 3:22-4:1
Titus 2:1-8		Titus 2:9, 10
I Peter 3:1-7		I Peter 2:18-25

One ancient non-Christian thinker named Epictetus (*eh-pik-TEET-us*) about A.D. 100 said, "I want . . . as a god-fearing man, a philosopher, and a diligent student, to know what is my duty toward the gods, toward parents, toward brothers, toward my country, toward strangers."[1] What Epictetus wanted Paul provided basically in Colossians 3:18—4:1.

The Christian Marriage

So, what is the difference between these Christian commands and similar ancient non-Christian codes? It is their stress upon *reciprocal* responsibility. These instructions seemed to be saying for each individual involved: I respect you and you are to be reciprocally responsible in your relationships with others. The ancient thinker Seneca said that "some have allowed only that part of philosophy which . . . tells the husband how to behave toward his wife, the father how to bring up his children, the master how to govern his slaves."[2] By contrast with those kinds of codes, Paul's was not one-sided and upper-sided only. Consequently, some people who might feel that some of Paul's urgings now seem antiquated or quaint should remind themselves how advanced they were for the time in which Paul was writing them.

Several overall observations may be made about Colossians 3:18—4:1. First, these principles operate most workably when people don't open mail not addressed to them. Macho husbands usually make trouble for themselves by trying to browbeat their wives to "submit." That piece of advice is not addressed to them but to "wives" (3:18). Furthermore, manipulative wives make little headway by nagging their husbands to "love." That piece of advice is not addressed to them but to "husbands" (3:19). It is improper to open mail that is not addressed to you!

Second, Paul's exhortations reveal an advance upon the standards of that time. As a Jew Paul had undoubtedly thanked God each morning that he was not made a Gentile, a slave, or a woman. But his command to "love" demands respectful treatment by the Christian husband.

J. B. Phillips's rendering of Colossians 3:18 and 19 says: "Wives, adapt yourselves to your husbands . . . Husbands, give your wives much love." There is nothing here to indicate that females are inferior to males. In the parallel counterpart to Colossians 3 in Ephesians 5 the apostle Paul launched into his remarks on reciprocal relationships by a preface to *all* groups: "Submit to one another out of reverence for Christ" (5:21).

 Janet complains that Ted never really listens to her and won't ever take her and their three children for family outings. Ted says that Janet dumps her problems on him the minute he walks in the door, worn out after work. How could Colossians 3:18 and 19 help Ted and Janet?

? What do you think "adapt"ing involves? What do you think "love" entails?

To "submit" in Colossians 3:18 has been interpreted in two basic ways. One way is to view it as a voluntary adaptation distinctive to the role relationship of the wife. A second way is to treat it as a carry-over from the flexible way any Christian should treat another Christian (by comparing Eph. 5:22 with Eph. 5:21).

A wife came to an Australian pastor with a problem. Her husband was beating her brutally. She asked the pastor for advice about what she should do. The pastor turned to Ephesians and Colossians and told her to go home and "submit." She did. Later she was beaten to death.

? Do you think Paul's admonitions apply in all cases? If not, what guidelines would you offer to modify them?

The apostle's admonition to husbands (3:19) is not: "Make sure you are the head of your homes." It is: "husbands love your wives." This is not mush, slush, and gush. This is a workable, work-at-it, responsible response. Ronald Ward, in commenting on the three Greek words available for Paul to use, noted (in oversimplification) that:

> *erao* is all take,
> *phileo* is give and take, and
> *agapao* is all give.
> (*Royal Sacrament*, p. 59)

Here it will be helpful to note what love does *not* involve:

1. cutting down one's spouse in public, or making derogatory jokes;
2. doing things that the husband may think are loving (e.g., bringing flowers) while neglecting what the other person needs (e.g., spending time listening to one's wife);
3. creating a TV football widow.

Colossians 3:19 adds for husbands: "do not be harsh with them [i.e., your wives]. The insensitive tactics of an Andy Capp or Hagar the Horrible of the comic strips are all too often only a caricature of the real daily happenings in homes. "It is useless to call your wife 'honey' if you act like vinegar toward her."[3]

The King James Version uses the word "bitter" for the NIV's translation "harsh." Bitterness builds up in a marriage when a spouse feels that his or her legitimate needs are not being met. Then that person buries those feelings instead of discussing them.

Are there any bitter feelings toward your marriage partner (or another person, if you are unmarried)? If so, how can you begin to confront those feelings constructively?

The Christian Family

Next, Paul shifts from marriage partners to family members.

 Do you think a child can and should obey a parent who is abusive?

The same word "fathers" in Colossians 3:21 is translated "parents" in Hebrews 11:23. Thus it would not be wrong to apply this verse to both parents. Consider the comments of leaders in the psychological field, quoted in excerpts below.

> I regard this [i.e., parenting] as the hardest, most complicated, anxiety-ridden, sweat and blood producing job in the world. It requires the ultimate in patience, common sense, commitment, honor, tact, love, wisdom, awareness and knowledge. At the same time, it holds the possibility for the most rewarding, joyous experience of a lifetime.
> —Virginia Satir, Peoplemaking

> Based on his research into the emotional needs of children in American families, Dr. Armand Nicoli, a psychologist at Harvard University, made this startling conclusion. Parents in the U.S. are more inaccesible to their children than parents in any other country in the world.
> —George Rekers, in Innovations

 There is a great difference between demanding and commanding respect.
> —Ralph Turnbull, A Minister's Obstacles

Parenthood is the art of bringing up children without putting them down.
> —Franklin Jones, in Growing Together

 What are some ways parents can cause their children to "become discouraged" (Col. 3:21) or get "an inferiority complex"?

Some possible answers might be:
1. Burying oneself in a newspaper and regularly giving a child the brush-off;
2. Grilling a child or youth with 20 questions whenever he or she comes back from outside the home;

70

3. "Why are you so stupid?" or "When will you ever learn?"
   (ingraining a fixation that they really are stupid);
4. Not affirming a child for doing good things, while badgering
   him or her about the bad things;
5. Embarrassing the child in front of other adults or the child's
   friends.

Contrast the two illustrations of family life listed below.

"My father, by his kindliness of manner and winning ways, made the heartstrings of his children twine around him . . . and deserved my lasting gratitude." Thus wrote David Livingstone, well-known missionary to Africa, of his father—who lived in a tenement, worked in a factory, taught Sunday school, and read everthing about missionaries that he could get his hands on. Livingstone's father was obviously not "the drill-instructor type of father" (as Dennis Guernsey labeled such a person in *The Family Covenant*).

Contrast the preceding story with one of a little girl who was an orphan, raised by her religious relatives. "Every move she made was subject to careful analysis by this clan of cranks. The slightest deviation was trumpeted as a wicked sin against the all-seeing eye of the never-sleeping God. Almost daily she was admonished to pledge not to drink, smoke, or swear. Four or five times a week the child was herded to church. At home she had to scrub floors and wash dishes before she was six. When she attempted to play act, a child's normal way to act out her childish fantasies, she was told with rigid implacability that she was sinning against God. Later in life feelings of guilt clung to her like barnacles to a sea-wall." Her name—Marilyn Monroe.

—Jess Moody, *You Can't Lose for Winning*

For "do not embitter," J.B. Phillips has "don't overcorrect your children" (3:21). Commentator John Eadie said wisely, "The twig is to be bent with caution."[4]

How do you think one should respond to the school of thought that says, "A child's will must be broken"?

The expression "become discouraged" is found in Greek only here in the New Testament. James Moffatt used the excellent choice of words, "dispirited," to translate it. "Few people would set out to teach a child that he [or she] is stupid, a bother, or unimportant. But when adults insist on doing things for the child, fail to praise his [or her] accomplishments, deride him [or her] for his failings, sigh when he [or she] wants something, and never have time for him; the child learns the lesson well."[5]

Slaves and Masters

The third pair of instructions pertains to slaves/masters (3:22—4:1).

 What do you notice about the amount of verses devoted to this subject in contrast to the preceding two sets of persons? Why is this?

In Bible times, slaves were attached to the household. Colossians 4:9, coupled with Philemon 8-21, shows that the Colosse church was facing a touchy slave-master issue: Onesimus and Philemon. Onesimus had been like the prodigal son in Luke 15—a runaway. In Colossians and Philemon, Onesimus becomes a returnee. How would this fragile situation be handled? Would the other Christian slaves there feel that Onesimus had been shown favoritism? Thus, the stay-at-home slaves might have felt like the elder brother in the story of the prodigal son.

PRODIGAL SON

ONESIMUS RETURNS

Paul the Wordsmith

Paul seemed to enjoy minting or making up his own words, for his writings are pimentoed (a verb you probably won't find in the dictionary) with vocabulary not found in any other Greek writings up to that point. One of these rare expressions, translated "when their eye is on you" by the NIV, is found only in Colossians 3:22 and Ephesians 6:6 (the parallel passage). Therefore, Paul may have coined this term by pasting together two other words. Similarly, the expression "to win their favor" is likewise found only here and in Ephesians 6:6.

 A maid was once asked how she knew she had really become a Christian. She replied, 'I know I am a Christian because I sweep under the rugs now!"

As an illustration of those who "try to win . . . favor" in the wrong way, an ancient writer, Dio Chrysostom, said of the group of Sophists: "They move always in the direction of the clapping and shouting."[6] By contrast, Paul called for "sincerity of heart" (3:22).

Colossians 3:23 is very similar to Colossians 3:17. Colossians 3:23 could be affixed over George Mueller's life, of whom it was said: "He brought everything to God, and brought God into everything."

Following the two rare words of Colossians 3:22 comes a word in 3:24 that is found only here in the Greek New Testament. This word (*antapodosis*) is probably a pun, because a slave might more readily expect *antapodoma*, found and translated in Romans 11:9 as "retribution." Instead of retribution, there is a reward; instead of punishment, a prize. And—surprise of surprises—what slave could expect to "receive an inheritance" (3:24)? Sons received inheritances, not slaves.

As if to counter any flak Philemon might receive from other slaves because of the returned runaway, Onesimus, Paul laid down the axiom: "Anyone who does wrong will be repaid for his wrong . . . ." (Col. 3:25). Interestingly, the very same verb in Greek is found concerning Onesimus in Philemon 18 ("If he has done you any wrong"). The final word in Colossians 3:25—"favoritism"—may be yet another word coined by Paul, and it softens the notion that runaways will get away with murder. These comments are significant, for a great many (perhaps a majority!) of the early Christians were slaves.

 Robert Ingersoll (1833-1899) said: "I would like to see a fair division of profits between capital and labor, so that the toiler could save enough to mingle a little June with the December of his life."
—in Laurence J. Peter, *Peter's Quotations*

With the first part of Ingersoll's comment, the apostle Paul stands unquestionably in agreement, calling for masters to "provide your slaves with what is right and fair" (or "fair and square").

How can an employer determine whether or not what he or she is paying employees is "right and fair"?

Many transfer the application of Colossians 3:22—4:1 to employees and employers. Suppose your boss, Mr. Phipps, is unfair, devious, and overbearing. Does the passage offer any consolation in coping with an irresponsible or immoral boss?

It is not always immediately possible to wriggle out of life's unpleasant job situations (cf. I Cor. 7:20-23). Consequently, employ the kit of helpful hints offered by 3:22—4:1, as follows:

- Give a 100 percent effort (3:22, 23).
- Rivet your attention on your real Boss (3:23, 24).
- Remember that wrongdoing will ultimately boomerang (3:25).

Turn the tables now and discuss "what is right and fair" (4:1) for a Christian employer—

- who hires a recent refugee for less than the minimum wage.
- who pays a woman running a Christian bookstore less than a male employee who works for her.
- who is a church choir director and regularly hands out photocopies of copyrighted sheet music.

The Apostle's Additional Advice to All (4:2-6)

After Paul has peeled off, as it were, layer after social layer, he now proceeds to counsel the complete Christian church at Colosse (4:2-6)

Ω The Greek word behind "devote yourselves" (or "continue," KJV) is found ten times in the Greek New Testament (in *Young's Analytical Concordance of the Bible* on page 201, columns 2 and 3, and page 87 in the back index to the New Testament; or page 218 [entry number 4342] in *Strong's Exhaustive Concordance of the Bible* will send you back to page 61 in its back index for all the English ways that this one Greek word is translated).

F. W. Beare mentions an illuminating usage of the same Greek verb outside the Bible when he says, "The verb . . . is . . . picturesque. It is used by the [Greek] historian Polybius to describe the obstinate continuance of a siege."[7] Just as troops would tenaciously persist in sieging a fortress, we are to persist tenaciously in prayer.

Note that Paul did not ask prayer for God to open the doors of his imprisonment, but for the Colossian Christians to pray that God would open "a door for our message" (4:3). Paul was frequently in stocks and bonds (heh! heh!), but the long-term value of his interests paid higher dividends. Interestingly, Curtis Mitchell claimed, "Neither Jesus nor Paul ever commanded us" to pray for the salvation of a lost soul. "The most explicit New Testament prayer for the unsaved is Paul's" in Romans 10:1.[8] However, in Colossians 4:3 Paul sought prayer for himself as he communicated with non-Christians.

The wise individual will "make the most of every opportunity" (Col. 4:5). John Broadus stated that "opportunity was like a fleet horse that pauses for one moment by one's side. If you fail to mount him in that moment, you can hear the clatter of his hoofs down the corridors of time."[9] In the same vein Captain Smollett in *Treasure Island* proposed to "take time by the forelock." Indeed, Ronald Ward paraphrases the phrase in Colossians 4:5, "cornering the market in opportunity"[10] [since the *agora*, marketplace, is built into the root-stock of this verb].

Within your normal week-time schedule what would be your "prime time" for making the most of your opportunities with reference to non-Christians?

A Christian's speech is to be peppered with grace and "seasoned with salt" (4:6).

 If we would win some, we must be winsome.
—Herbert Lockyer, *Evangelize or Fossilize*
We must win the people to us first, then we can win them to Christ.
—D. L. Moody, in Richard Curtis, *They Called Him Mr. Moody*
You will always catch more flies with sugar than with vinegar.
—C. H. Spurgeon, *The Pastor and His Work*

The preceding quotations provide cues on speaking with grace. In classical Greek "grace" had the connotation of "pleasing" or "attractiveness." Thus, cactus Christians, or cockleburr Christians, with prickly pear personalities, have deep lessons to learn.

 What are some spin-off implications of being "seasoned with salt"?

The salt metaphor may imply such things as: (1) zest, tartness, spiciness; (2) wit (the bad connotation of this word is found in *salacious* stories, a word similar to the word *saline*); (3) using good sense (try using too much salt on a potato and you'll wish you hadn't); (4) preserving purity and preventing putrefaction (what we do for meat with the modern refrigerator, the ancients accomplished with salt).

The last meaning probably comes closest to Paul's actual intention, as demonstrated by setting Colossians 4:6 beside its companion statement in Ephesians 4:29.

COLOSSIANS 4:6	EPHESIANS 4:29
"Let your conversation be always full of *grace*,	"Let no *corrupt* communication proceed out of
seasoned with *salt*"	your mouth . . . that it may minister *grace* unto the hearers" (KJV)

Therefore, grace-full conversation is salt-seasoned; it acts as a preventative of corruption.

Chapter 8 will be Paul's spice rack, detailing the numerous personalities who spiced his own life.

8

MEMORABLE MEMOS

Colossians 4:7-18

Whoabouts is not a word you will find in the dictionary. *Whereabouts*—yes; *whoabouts*—no. Although we assume that Paul was under house arrest in Rome (Acts 28) when he wrote Colossians, we cannot be absolutely certain of his whereabouts, for all we know is that he was somewhere in chains (Col. 4:18). However, though we cannot tell for certain about his whereabouts, we can say some things for certain about his *whoabouts*—that is, the people about whom he was mentally occupied at that point. In a memorable memo in Colossians 4:7-18 Paul named ten people who were concerned with him or the Colossian church.

NAMES COMPARED

Vs.	Colossians 4	Vs.	Philemon
9	Onesimus	10	Onesumus
10	Mark	24	Mark
10	Aristarchus	24	Aristarchus
11	Jesus Justus	23	Jesus (?)
12	Luke	24	Luke
14	Demas	24	Demas
17	Archippus	2	Archippus

Because seven of the ten names in Colossians 4:7-17 appear in Philemon, we would assume that the two letters were being sent to the same location, even if we did not have further information. It is essentially the same cast of characters.

Ironically, in both Romans (16) and Colossians (4) there are long lists of names despite the probablity that Paul had personally visited neither church (Rom. 1:10-13; Col. 2:1). Leon Morris explained: "When he is writing to a church he knows, Paul does not usually send many greetings (which may create ill will); but when, as here, he writes to a church he has not visited, he not uncommonly sends a number of greetings."[1]

I. TWO LETTER CARRIERS: TYCHICUS AND ONESIMUS (4:7-9)

Four Phases of Tychicus's Tale

Tychicus (*TICK-ih-kus*) crops up in five New Testament passages relating to four different spots in Paul's life. Notice that when you read about Tychicus, he is traveling with or for Paul.

1. About A.D. 57 Tychicus was part of the traveling team on Paul's third missionary journey. He was one of seven of the apostle's accompanists from Macedonia, i.e., modern Greece (Acts 20: 4), who presumably carried the money collection from Gentile churches to the impoverished Jewish church in Jerusalem. From there the group travelled to Troas in Asia Minor, near the tip of Europe (Acts 20:5; cf. 16:8-10). Tychicus was a native of the province of Asia.

2. About A.D. 60-63 (three to six years later) we find Tychicus in the companion epistles of Ephesians (6:21) and Colossians (4:7). In both texts he appears to be a news taker and news teller. Evidently he was one of the couriers to the Colossians (4:8) from Paul. Consequently, it is to this relatively unknown man—whom you may not have even known before this study—that we owe the preservation of three books of our New Testament, for most probably Tychicus was a mail carrier for Ephesians, Colossians, and Philemon!

3. About A.D. 66 or 67 Tychicus may have functioned as a replacement for Titus on the island of Crete (Tit. 3:12).

4. About A.D. 68 Tychicus apparently served as a replacement for Timothy at Ephesus near the coast of Asia Minor (II Tim. 4:12). Thus, Tychicus appears to have been one of Paul's faithful cohorts in both his imprisonments.

 From the three titles in Colossians 4:7 and the composite picture in the New Testament, what qualities would you ascribe to Tychicus and who do you know who is like him?

Onesimus

Both in Colossians and Philemon Archippus and Onesimus (*oh-NESS-ih-muss*) are named outside the formal list of greetings. Onesimus, the formerly useless slave who is the subject of the Letter to Philemon, will be treated in chapters 11 and 12. Probably in Rome, over 1000 miles from his home base, his path intersected with Paul's, and he was converted. Note that this slave is joined with a free man ("they," 4:9) as having a story to tell.

II. THREE JEWISH STALWARTS: ARISTARCHUS, MARK, AND JESUS JUSTUS (4:10, 11)

Aristarchus—Collection Companion

Like Tychicus, Aristarchus (air-ih-STAR-kus) appears in five New Testament passages (Acts 19:29; 20:4; 27:2; Col. 4:10; Philem. 24).

1. Along with Gaius, Aristarchus was seized in Ephesus during the riot there on Paul's third missionary journey (Acts 19:29).

2. Along with Secundus of Thessalonica, Aristarchus was one of the seven collection carriers traveling with Paul on his third missionary journey.

3. We know that Aristarchus was with Paul when his ship to Rome embarked (Acts 27:2) and we find him with Paul in Rome. But whether he was by his side during all the in-between time, we don't know. Sir William Ramsay, the archaeologist, held that in order to accompany Paul the prisoner legally, Aristarchus would have had to serve as his slave.[2] This would be an interesting turn of events, since Aristarchus name means best ruler (arist- as in aristocrat, arch- as in anarchy, oligarchy, monarchy, etc.). Whether Ramsay's idea is true, it is true that real greatness lies in servanthood (Mt. 20:26).

The term "fellow prisoner" woodenly means "fellow prisoner of war" (4:10), although it is probable that we should not take it literally. Paul and his companions are spiritual Christ-captives. Perhaps Aristarchus and Epaphras took turns sharing Paul's imprisonment.

Mark—Paradigm of Restoration

Mark's biography can be pieced together from Acts 12:12, 25; 13:5, 13; 15:36-39; Colossians 4:10; II Timothy 4:11; Philemon 24; I Peter 5:13. Perhaps Mark was one of those "not many [Christians who] were of noble birth" (I Cor. 1:26). The home of his mother had served as the hub of early Jerusalem Christians (Acts 12:12). He had the Jewish name John and took the Latin name Marcus. Mark joined Paul and Barnabas on their first missionary journey (Acts 13:5) as an assistant or apprentice. For some reason he went A.W.O.L. (Acts 13:13). When Barnabas, Mark's cousin (Col. 4:10), wanted to take Mark again on the second missionary journey, "a sharp clash of opinion" (Acts 15:39,

J. B. Phillips) resulted between Barnabas and Paul. Consequently, "Barnabas took Mark and sailed for Cyprus" (Acts 15:39).

 What can be learned from the falling out between Barnabas and Paul?

The argument between Paul and Barnabas occurred about A.D. 50. From that point a curtain of silence is drawn over Mark's activities for about 12 years. The next notice served of him is found in Colossians 4:10 and Philemon 24 where Paul had evidently come to a revised version of John Mark. Any vapors of doubt are blown away in II Timothy 4:11 (about A.D. 68). Thus, Mark serves as a paradigm of restoration. A Christian need not slump under the banner of "Once Failure, Always Failure."

 How is Mark's biography a reassurance to you?

Jesus Justus—a Therapeutic Friend

There were numerous Jesuses in Bible times. (*Jesus* is the Greek equivalent for the Hebrew *Joshua.*) This character, found only here in the Bible, had the Greek form of the Jewish name of Jesus and the Latin name of Justus. (The name "Justus" is given to two other New Testament individuals; Acts 1:23; 18:7.)

 Has anyone ever functioned like some kind of medicine toward you? What type of medicine does that person remind you of, and why?
Paul said of his co-workers for the Kingdom of God (including Jesus Justus) that they proved a "comfort" to him (4:11). The word "comfort" is fascinating. It is found only here in the Greek New Testament. The Greek is *paregoria*, from which we derive the English "paregoric." Paregoric is a form of medicine. *Webster's New Collegiate Dictionary* says paregoric is "camphorized tincture of opium." By itself it is poisonous, but if diluted in considerable water it becomes a pain-reliever.
Some people function therapeutically or medicinally in our lives. One might think, "As a teacher I remember the day my classroom was my headache. It was parents' night and I had a lot to clean up. But Norma was my aspirin. She volunteered to help me clean the room."
Has your life had any pain-reliever people? Any "uppers"? Any Christians who act like sedatives for you? (Unfortunately, some may serve as pain inducers rather than pain relievers!) "A cheerful heart is good medicine" (Prov. 17:22). For whom could you be good therapy this week?

Amazingly, the three previously named individuals were "the only Jewish Christians in Rome of any prominence who . . . stood by [Paul] as co-workers."[3]

 Has some Christian stuck by you through thick and thin? If so, what were the circumstances that endeared you to that person?

III. THREE GENTILE CO-WORKERS: EPAPHRAS, LUKE, AND DEMAS (4:12-14)

Epaphras

Epaphras (*EP-uh-fruss*) is mentioned in Colossians 1:7, 8; 4:12, 13; and Philemon 23. He is generally considered the founding father and pioneering pastor of the Colossian church. He may have been a convert of Paul during the evangelism that radiated from Ephesus (about 100 miles away) for several years (Acts 19:10).

Epaphras was undoubtedly Paul's informant concerning the Colossian heresy. The expression "one of you" (4:12) brands him as a Colosse resident. It is interesting that while Paul did not here call Onesimus (the slave) a slave (4:9)—as if to elevate his stature back home—Paul did call Epaphras, the church founder, a "servant [or slave] of Christ Jesus" (4:12).

F. W. Beare noted, "The verb ["wrestling"], originally used of contesting for the prize in games of track and field, had been extended metaphorically by classical writers to describe struggles for the supreme issues of life."[4]

 Paul employed sports contests to illustrate spiritual experience. What other illustrations from modern life can be used to illustrate Christian experience?

Of all Paul's helpers, Epaphras is the only one so commended for his prayers. Epaphras was Paul's student in the school of prayer.

 What do you think is involved in "wrestling in prayer" (4:12)? How can you incorporate this into your own prayer life?

Paul vouched that Epaphras was "working hard" (4:13) for the tri-city Christians. Certainly, if he had made a trip of over a thousand miles to Rome, Epaphras was no slouch.

Laodicea and Hierapolis

Two neighbor towns of Colosse are mentioned in Colossians 4:13. We might say that Laodicea, Hierapolis, and Colosse formed the tri-cities in the Lycus River valley in western Asia Minor. (See map, page 9.)

 Where else have you heard of the church of the Laodiceans in the New Testament? (Check a Bible concordance if necessary.) By reading that New Testament passage on the church in Laodicea, can you see any parallels to the spiritual climate at Colosse as found in Colossians?

A major Roman highway ran through Asia Minor from the Euphrates to Ephesus (on the west coast) and followed along the Meander River valley in western Asia Minor. Whether Paul stopped at any of the three cities during his travels is not certain, although Colossians 2:1 seems to rule out any long-term encounter with Christians at Colosse. Laodicea (addressed in Rev. 3:14-22) was located about ten miles northwest of Colosse.

Laodicea was named for Laodice, wife of Antiochus II of Syria (261-247 B.C.). Laodicea was a banking center, where the Roman statesman Cicero once stopped to get some cash. It was also renowned for the glossy black wool of local sheep (cp. Rev. 3:18). The Laodiceans are remembered as the lukewarm church of Revelation 3.

Hierapolis (meaning "holy city") was approximately six miles north of Laodicea and about thirteen miles northwest of Colosse. Upon exiting from Laodicea one could see the whitened cliffs toward Hierapolis. William Hendriksen wrote that Hierapolis "stood over a lofty terrace. Over the precipitous cliffs which support this terrace glistening cataracts of pure white stone, the chalky deposits of the streams, came tumbling down into the plain below. In the autumn these frozen falls, glistening in the sunlight and visible from a distance, afford a beautiful sight."[5] These chalky cliffs are called by the natives the "Castle of Cotton."[6]

The area at Hierapolis was also something like Hot Springs, Arkansas, producing mysterious vapors that made it: (1) on the one hand, a city of "self-made baths," and (2) on the other hand, a sort of religious shrine for superstitious ancient people.

Luke

In *Treasure Island* Dr. Livesey is the cautious, sane, courageous, powdered-wigged gentleman who (as magistrate) puts ex-pirate Billy Bones in his place and sails away with Jim Hawkins as his protector to locate buried treasure. In that story he might be called a "dear friend" and "the doctor" (Col. 4:14). For Paul, out of all those who sent greetings, Luke is the "dear friend."

This is the only place in the New Testament where Luke is labeled a doctor (4:14). Furthermore, it is largely assumed from this passage that Luke was the only Gentile author of the New Testament. This is because Paul had just previously bracketed three other friends together (in 4:10, 11) as being "the only Jews" who stuck like adhesive to him while he was under that arrest. Interestingly, Luke and Demas are joined together in three passages—here; II Timothy 4:10,11; and Philemon 24. Indeed, apart from the later headings over Luke's Gospel and Acts, those are the only three spots in the New Testament where Luke's name occurs.

What did it mean to be a medical doctor in those days? "Surgeons performed operations on the skull, tracheotomies (incisions into the windpipe), and amputations. A variety of medical instruments were used, such as lancets, stitching needles, an elevator for lifting up depressed portions of the skull, different kinds of forceps, catheters, spatulas for examining the throat . . . ."[7]

 It is said that a clergyman sees [people] at their best, a lawyer at their worst, and a doctor as they are.
     —William Barclay, *Introduction to the First Three Gospels*

 What doctorly traits would make Luke an ideal gospel writer (see Luke 1:1-4) and friend for Paul?

Demas

 How does Demas compare with the first seven people mentioned in Colossians 4:7-14? How would you contrast the Demas of II Timothy 4:10 with the Mark of II Timothy 4:11? How are the Demas and Mark of II Timothy 4 like Judas and Peter?

Unlike practically all of the seven preceding people in Colossians 4:7-14, Demas receives no special compliment. In light of II Timothy 4:11 (written probably four to eight years after Colossians), could Paul's silence about Demas in Colossians 4:14 be a telltale commentary? Could Paul have had little worthwhile to say about Demas? Could their relationship have been cooling? Could Demas have already been exhibiting giveaway clues as to his long-range character? At any rate, by the time of Paul's last preserved letter, Demas had defected.

 What signs do you look for that someone is about to become a church dropout?

IV. TWO LOCAL CHRISTIANS: NYMPHA AND ARCHIPPUS (4:15-17)

Nympha

Some ancient Greek manuscripts have Nymphas (so KJV, LB)—a male, whereas other Greek manuscripts have the word Nympha—a female. The majority of modern translations (NIV, NEB, MLB, RSV, GNB, NASB, J.B. Phillips, etc.) feel that the weight of manuscript evidence favors a female, Nympha.

Nympha hosted a house church. Church buildings did not crop up until after New Testament times. Archaeologists have excavated a house at Dura-Europos on the Euphrates River where an ordinary house was enlarged and redesigned to accommodate a church. The New Testament names a number of house churches (e.g., in Gaius's house at Corinth, Rom. 16:23; in Philemon's house, Philem. 2).

In Colossians 4:16 Paul calls for an interchurch exchange of letters. Some of the views about the letter in Colossians 4:16 are that it was a:

(1) letter from Laodicea to Paul (John Calvin);
(2) letter from Laodicea by Paul;
(3) letter to Laodicea from Paul.

The third view seems to be the case. But if so, what happened to it? The "letter from Laodicea" was either (1) lost (like the real I Corinthians—see I Cor. 5:9; II Cor. 7:8), or (2) it may actually be our canonical Epistle to the Ephesians. This is possible because many Greek manuscripts omit "at Ephesus" from Ephesians 1:1, and the letter is very general as compared with Colossians. (There was a forged, apocryphal Epistle to the Laodiceans—a sort of mosaic of Paul-like writings—rejected by Jerome around A.D. 300 and reprimanded by the council of Nicea in A.D. 787.)

Archippus

Our total information (but like Old Mother Hubbard's cupboard it is rather bare) on Archippus (ar-KIP-us) is found in Colossians 4:17 and Philemon 2. Probably Archippus was Philemon's son (Philem. 2) and was pastoring in that region (Col. 4:17). His efforts in the Lycus River Valley would be even more strategic during Epaphras's absence. Tradition holds that Archippus was stoned to death with Philemon.

 Look again at Paul's word-tribute to the ten Christians in Colossians 4:7-17. Who in your realm of acquaintances might you write a note of thanks to, or express verbal appreciation toward?

In some locations it would appear that spurious letters had been circulated in Paul's name (II Thess. 2:2). Consequently, even when he used an amanuensis, or secretary, Paul might sign off with his own distinctive signature (I Cor. 16:21; Col. 4:18; II Thess. 3:17) to protect against forgery. Some have surmised that he wrote with extra-large letters in Galatians 6:11, because he had unusual eye trouble (Gal. 4:15). Tertius (TUR-shus) was one secretary Paul named. Tertius penned Romans (16:22) as Paul dictated.

Colossians closes on an emotionally touching note, as Paul urges the readers to "remember my chains" (Col. 4:18). A. T. Robertson imagines, "here he could probably not go on, for the hand of the Roman soldier jerked him away."[8] Whether it happened quite that way or not, the basic point is still valid.

 Can you recall being moved emotionally at the plight or remark of another Christian?

Colossians 4:18 is Paul's shortest closing prayer. (See II Cor. 13:14 for the longest.) Just as Paul opened the letter with his trademark ("grace," Col. 1:2), even so he closes with the word of which he never tired, the fabulous word that served as his logo and his liberator (II Cor. 8:9; I Tim. 1:14, 15). Paul signed off in Romans (16:24); I Corinthians (16:23); II Corinthians (13:14); Galatians (6:18); Ephesians (6:24); Philippians (4:23); Colossians (4:18); I Thessalonians (5:28); II Thessalonians (3:18); II Timothy (4:22); Titus (3:15); and Philemon (25) with "grace." Only I Timothy is missing Paul's earmark. What golden arches are to the McDonalds restaurant chain, what a blimp is to Goodyear, what the Rock of Gibraltar is to Prudential insurance—"grace" is to Paul. He was graced. We are graced. Thanks be to God, and grace to you, too!

 If your friends, neighbors, or co-workers were asked to pick out a trademark for you, what do you think it would be?

Anchors Aweigh!

In Robert Louis Stevenson's *Treasure Island*, the pirate Billy Bones had been terrorizing the clientele at the Admiral Benbow Inn. Then Dr. Livesey, the country gentleman and magistrate in powdered wig, visited the inn.

That evening Cap'n Bones wildly ordered silence from the patrons of the Admiral Benbow, but the good doctor failed to comply. Bones pulled a knife on him. Dr. Livesey calmly told the seafaring scarecrow

84

that if he didn't sheath his knife, he'd see to it that Bones took part in the next hanging. After a battle of stares, the menacing pirate retreated.

Dr. Livesey, Squire Trelawney, Captain Smollett, and Jim Hawkins are names encased in childhood's memory chest as part of the valiant crew of the ship *Hispaniola*. That other real-life sea traveler, the apostle Paul, also commanded a valiant crew against the harassing of philosophical pirates at Colosse. Only Paul had to operate, one might say, from a remote control command post (Col. 2:1), for the power this treasured letter wields over 1,900 years later came from a man who was in chains (4:18).

The final section of Colossians (4:7-18) consists of personal memos, as it were, from our sea captain's journal. Paul's crew of faithful hands in Colossians 4:7-18 teaches us:

(1) That we may not necessarily have many tried-and-true friends;
(2) That one may end life for Christ without having a vast reservoir of friends;
(3) That God gives us some "adhesive" Christians when we really need them.

. . . And so, mates, it's been good having you aboard ship in search of buried treasure. Keep a sailor's eye peeled on the horizon for any philosophical pirates who would threaten to take you captive (Col. 2:8). And, finally, enjoy "the glorious riches of this mystery, which is Christ in you, the hope of glory" (Col. 1:27).

9

COLOSSIANS IN CAPSULE
Overview and Review

It's now time to hop into our mental helicopter and head up over the treetops of Colossians. We don't want to miss the total forest of Colossians because of having analyzed the individual trees. After our verse-by-verse *analysis* (breaking up into parts) of Colossians in the first eight chapters in this study book, this chapter is devoted to a thematic *synthesis* (putting together in a whole) of Colossians.

First, we will present the overall outline in brief for our surveillance. Secondly, we will consider the reason Colossians was written. Thirdly, we will survey in more detail the overview of Colossians from the standpoint of the reason it was written. Here is the condensed outline:

I. *Opening Greetings and Gratitude (1:1-11)*
   A. The Greetings He Relays (1:1, 2)
   B. The Gratitude He Relates (1:3-8)
   C. The Goals He Requests (1:9-11)

II. *A Theology to Treasure (1:12—2:7)*
   Here Christ is viewed as containing "the fullness of the Deity" (2:9; cf. 1:19) rather than seeing that fullness conveyed through elemental spirits of the universe, or angels (2:18). Christ "reconcile[d] all things"(1:20); therefore, "he has reconciled you," Paul concludes in 1:22. Our Lord is above all angels. He disarmed angelic powers (2:15) in death of any possible control over humanity's destiny. Thus, this unit presents Christ as Reconciler of all.
   A. The Shift to Reconciliation (1:12-14): "he has rescued us from the dominion of darkness" (1:13).

B. The Hymn Celebrating Reconciliation (1:15-20): Christ "reconcile[d] . . . all things," including "thrones or powers or rulers or authorities" (i.e., angels; 1:16).
C. The Colossians Involved in Reconciliation—as objects (1:21-23a): "he has reconciled you" (1:22).
D. Paul Involved in Reconciliation—as subject (1:23b—2:7): "of which I, Paul, have become a servant" (1:23).

III. *A Life-Style to Live (2:8—4:6)*
If in the first main section of Colossians Christ is Lord above angels, in this second section "Christ . . . is your life" (3:4) beyond asceticism.
A. This Life-Style Is Not Based on False "Philosophy" (2:8-15)
B. This Life-Style Is Not Regulated by Ascetic Regulations (2:16—3:4)
C. This Life-Style Is Characterized by Heaven-on-Earth Character (3:5-17)
D. This Life-Style Is Practiced in Down-to-Earth Relationships (3:18—4:1)
E. This Life-Style Is Supported by Prayerful Wisdom (4:2-6)

IV. *Closing Greetings and Grace (4:7-18)*
Now that we've surveyed *what* Colossians is about, let's ask *why* it was written. There were apparently two explosive issues at the back of Paul's mind as he wrote: (1) opponents on the scene; (2) Onesimus's situation. The second fragile issue is handled primarily in the letter to Philemon, although its overtones are not absent toward the end of Colossians. (This will be dealt with in chapters 11 and 12 of this study guide on Philemon.)

The overarching positive concern Paul had for the Colossian Christian church triggered his negative concern to combat certain cultists who seemed to be a threat at Colosse. While the letter does not pinpoint what specific situation compelled Paul to write, we can pick up numerous clues about the book's background by reading between the lines. Just as a husband or wife can often reconstruct what's happening at the other end of the line by listening to his or her spouse's conversation on one end of the telephone, even so we can get a general picture of the face of the puzzle's boxtop by piecing together the fragments of the puzzle provided in the Letter to the Colossians. That there was some "hollow and deceptive philosophy" lurking in the Colossian region is apparent from Colossians 2:4 and 8. The vague, misty contours of this false philosophy are described most fully for us in

Colossians 2:16-23. However, there is no known heresy from the ancient world precisely like what is outlined in Colossians. That is why many scholars call the threat the "Colossian heresy."

Whatever the hideous head of this heretical monster looked like, certain contours of it are clear. Furthermore, Colossians is pimentoed with vocabulary that is known to scholars from cults (i.e., mystery religious and second century Gnosticism) in the ancient world. Here are some red-flag terms to look for as you read Colossians. They appear to be technical vocabulary that the local cultists used. Paul seems to have adopted and adapted some of these cultists' code words to use against them. Some of these red-flag, slogan words are:

- knowledge (1:9,10; 2:3);
- fullness (1:19; 2:9, 10);
- mystery (1:26, 27; 2:2);
- philosophy (2:8).

Thus, it is as if Paul blew up their false ideas with the dynamite of the Christian Gospel, but picked up the scraps and fragments of their own wordcraft and constructed his own missile to attack this sub-Christian, "higher life" religious philosophy. The opposed philosophy was "first-century scientology."[1]

Consider this cult from the standpoint of the *geography* of the region. Imagine that you were a primitive person who had stumbled for the first time upon the geysers of Yosemite National Park! What would you think? The region around Colosse was noted for its sulphurous springs and steaming mists. Superstitious ancients would think this was sacred ground to some gods. (In fact, from the *plutonium* of that region the god *Pluto* was worshipped.)

Not only was the region known from its mysterious springs, etc., but its Eastern expressway (from Ephesus to the Euphrates) imported Eastern esoteric and exotic ideas. Besides the *geography*, the *demography* (or statistical spread of the population) contributed to the mushrooming of cults. There were native Phrygians, Greek settlers, and Jewish immigrants who made up the composite, cosmopolitan composition of the population in the neighborhood of Colosse. Furthermore, people spoke about the Phrygian district in terms of strange religions in the same manner that U.S. people do about bizarre cults multiplying in Southern California.

While we cannot absolutely pinpoint the exact makeup of the cult at Colosse, we can safely say that it shared certain characteristics in common with second-century Gnosticism (*NAHS-tih-siz-um*). In its more fully flowered form Gnosticism (or Knowism, as it has been

labeled) displays certain characteristics. The chief characteristics of Gnosticism were:
- (1) The view that salvation comes through knowledge (Greek *gnosis*, pronounced *KNOW-sis*);
- (2) The view that what is physical is tainted with evil (i.e., our world and our bodies). This had important implications for Christ's earthly body, Christ's resurrection body, and the Christian's resurrection.

Because of some overlap between the first century Colossian cult and second century gnosticism, some will speak of the Colossian cult as a kind of proto-[or beginning] gnosticism [with a small g]. However we label it, we know that it was dangerous cult-cancer, ready to flourish within the doctrinal tissue of the developing church—if given the chance.

Now let's review Colossians as a whole in light of the cult attempting to infect the readers.

OUTLINED OVERVIEW

I. *Opening Greetings and Gratitude (1:1-11)*
- A. The Greetings He Relays (1:1, 2). Paul's opener follows the stereotyped formula for all his epistles. Paul was an "apostle" to the Colossian Christians just as he was an apostle to the Roman Gentile Christians (Rom. 1:5-7), despite the evidence that he had never visited either church group in person. It is probably important here for Paul to reinforce that he is an apostle "by the will of God" (1:1), since there were other religious ideas encroaching and competing for the Colossians' commitment.

  Paul was joined by Timothy (1:1) who would four to eight years later (in I and II Timothy) have to face similar heretical ideas at Ephesus (I Tim. 1:3), which was about one hundred miles from Colosse. Timothy would face "false doctrines" (I Tim. 1:3) "of what is falsely called knowledge" (I Tim. 6:20) involving a "down with the body and matter" campaign (I Tim. 4:3-5). Thankfully, those Christians at Colosse had remained "faithful" (1:2).
- B. The Gratitude He Relates (1:3-8). Paul wasn't grateful for any pseudo-intellectual knowledge the church had, but because of their faith and love (1:4). This came about because the Christian message came to them (1:5). Their response to the evangel (or Gospel) was reported by their evangelist,

Epaphras (1:8). Not only were the Colossian Christians "faithful" (1:2) to the truth, but Epaphras was "faithful" (1:7). Paul doesn't say that Epaphras tattled on the Colossians and that they were falling prey to an insidious cult. Instead, he attested: "All over the world this gospel is bearing fruit" (1:6). In other words, this is not some locally homegrown religious idiosyncrasy of cultists, but a Gospel for all. Their gnosticism was for the elite few.

C. The Goals He Requests (1:9-11). Paul had already indicated that the Colossian Christians "understood God's grace in all its truth" (1:6) rather than some gnostic heresy. He continued "asking God to fill you with the *knowledge* of his will through all spiritual *wisdom* and *understanding*" (1:9). The Knowists weren't the only ones in the know. By means of the three italicized knowledge-related terms immediately above, Paul prays that Christians will possess the true *gnosis*. In fact, he prays that they will have *gnosis* in its fullness ("full" was likely another cultist term).

Just as the "gospel is bearing fruit and growing" (1:6), so Paul prayed that they might be "bearing fruit . . . growing in the knowledge of God" (1:10). Authentic knowledge combats counterfeit knowledge.

Having opened verse 3 with "We always thank God," the body of Colossians now begins with "giving thanks" (1:12). These two terms of thanks are like slices of bread sandwiching the opening into one whole.

II. A *True Theology to Treasure* (1:12—2:7)
   A. The Shift to Reconciliation (1:12-14). In gnostic thought, Heaven and earth could never come together. But that is the subject Paul tackles, presenting Christ the reconciler. This is significant because Gnostics viewed the evil world as separated from a pure God and only bridged by a group of in-between emanations, i.e., aeons (or, as we might say: angels).

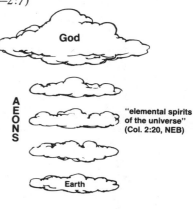

Paul doesn't buy this structuring of the universe, as if a stairstep world of angels bridged the gulf to God. No! Christ is reconciler, bridging the gulf.

Consequently, Paul shifts to this subject of reconciliation by saying that God:

"qualified you" (1:12);
"rescued us" (1:13);
"brought us into the kingdom" (1:13);
redeemed; and
forgave us (1:14).

At this juncture many Bible scholars feel that Paul pasted in, as it were, an early church hymn (Col. 1:15-20). This hymn said just what he wanted to say. Notice the shift from

"you" (vs. 12) and "us" (vs. 13)
to
no personal pronouns in verses 15-20
(other than "he" and "him")

back to "you" and "your" in verse 21.

B. The Hymn Celebrating Reconciliation (1:15-20). In this early Christian hymn we may view the structure: Christ is

Head over creation (1:15-17)
—"firstborn over all creation" (vs. 15)
and
Head over the church (1:18-20)
—"firstborn from among the dead" (vs. 18).

In contrast to all angelic administrators, "God was pleased to have all his fullness dwell" in Christ (1:19). In certain ancient Greek documents *pleroma*, or "fullness," is used for God. But in second century gnosticism the *pleroma* (*PLAY-row-mah*) is the whole body of angel-like emanations. Thus, Paul borrowed another of the cultists' code words ["fullness"] and rerouted it to his purpose.

Such cultists tended to be mystical, ethereal, other-worldly, far out. But Paul asserted the very down-to-earth, historically anchored assertion that Christ made "peace through his blood, shed on the cross" (1:20).

C. The Colossians Involved in Reconciliation —as Objects (1:21-23a).

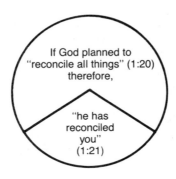

The "before" of verse 21 ("once") is offset by the "after" of verse 22 ("but now").

D. Paul Involved in Reconciliation—As Subject (1:23b—2:7). Whereas the Colossian Christians were *reconciled* to God, Paul was the active human agent involved in the *reconciling* process, the "servant" (1:23) triggering reconciliation. In Colossians 1:23:b—2:7 Paul:

    1. suffered on behalf of the readers (1:24);
    2. was a servant for them (1:25);
    3. was the "secret" proclaimer to them (1:26-28);
    4. was a costruggler with them (1:29; 2:1);
    5. was a site setter for them (2:2, 3); and
    6. was a signal giver to warn them (2:4-7).

Like the cultists, God has a secret (or "mystery"; 1:26, 27). Unlike any cultists, Paul's mystery is no supersecret for the select spiritual elite, the few who are in the know. His good news is "proclaimed to *every* creature under heaven" (1:23). Paul said, "We proclaim [Christ to] . . . *everyone . . . so that we may present everyone* perfect in Christ" (1:28). Beware of any minority element that acts like they've "got the secret"!

"In his . . . *Preface to Morals* (1929) Walter Lippmann . . . expressed the opinion that no great ancient teacher of . . . religion ever thought of teaching the highest wisdom to everybody. But this is just what Paul expressly sought to do [in Colossians 1:28]."[2]

In Colossians 1:28 Paul purposes to present his converts "perfect in Christ." "Perfect" was probably another heretical technical term used to describe the "initiated." But Paul wanted everyone initiated into the group of those who know the Good News experientially. Indeed, Paul continued by saying, "I want you [plural; that is, all of you as a group—in contrast to cultic elitism] to know" (2:1).

Just as Colossians 1:9 was peppered with words gnostics might have used ("knowledge," "wisdom," "understanding"), so also Colossians 2:2, 3 is pimentoed with more words cultists might have claimed as their peculiar property ("understanding, "know," "mystery," "hidden," "wisdom," "knowledge"). It almost sounds as if Paul had in front of him a copy of the cult's promotional brochures. The ancient mystery religions viewed *mysteries* as the entranceway to a secret lore. But Paul wanted his readers to "know the mystery of God, namely, Christ" (2:2). "If there *is* a secret, it is all in Christ."[3]

Christ is the open book, the public thesaurus of "hidden . . . knowledge" (2:3). An interesting passage appears in the Jewish Book of Enoch (about 70 B.C.): "This is the Son of Man who hath righteousness . . . and who revealeth all the treasures of that which is hidden."[4]

Some background for the practices of the ancient mystery religions is supplied by Lewis Johnson: "In them the initiate, after a long period of training and instruction, was allowed to be present at a . . . passion play. By means of the performance the initiate was to have an experience of identification with his god. To outsiders the ritual would have been a mystery."[5]

Paul was not ready to say, "This is a nice religious experience which is true for some but not for others." He wrote

"That no one may deceive you" (2:4) and
"That no one takes you captive" (2:8) and
"do not let anyone judge you" (2:16).

Paul labeled the adversaries' approach:

"fine-sounding arguments" (2:4) and
"hollow and deceptive philosophy" (2:8) and
"self-imposed worship—based on human commands" (2:22, 23).

Paul concluded this major section (1:12—2:7) by urging the Colossian church to continue in Christianity "just as you received Christ" (2:6). The word "received" is a technical term for transmitting tradition, such as the Colossian cultists would have done—as is evident from verse 2:8 ("deceptive philosophy, which depends on human tradition"). Just as Paul sandwiched 1:3-11 together with references to "thanks" (1:3, 12), so also 1:12—2:7 opens and closes "with thankfulness" (2:7).

III. *A Life-Style to Live (2:8—4:6)*

> In 1:12—2:7 Christ is Lord above angels.
> In 2:8—4:6 "Christ . . . is your life" above asceticism.

A. This Life-Style Is Not Based on False "Philosophy" (2:8-15). The heretics prided themselves in having "superknowledge," secrets, and traditions that no one else knew. Paul called such secretive lore "hollow" (2:8). The Greek word Paul used, *kenes* (ken-ACE), could be a take-off on one ancient name for the "untouchable God" of philosophy, *Kenoma* or Emptiness. Such terms as "hollow" (or empty) and "tradition" (2:8) are "perhaps a veiled glance at the secret transmission of formulae and passwords in the gnosticizing religion at Colosse."[6]

Such cult philosophy was regulated by "the elemental spirits of the universe" (2:8, NEB). (For a discussion of this important item see the heading "Angels" in chapter 10 of this study guide.)

In contrast to any cultic *Kenoma* (Emptiness—see immediately above), Christians possessed the opposite of "Emptiness"—namely, "fullness." In Colossians 2:9, 10 (which we might designate as the key verses to Colossians) Paul wrote:

> "in Christ all the *fullness* of the Deity lives
> and
> you have been given *fullness* in Christ."

"Fullness" (2:9, 10) was a term that some cult types used for either: (1) the God who had no direct contact with the earth (known as the Emptiness or *Kenoma*); or (2) that gulf of space between God and evil earth bridged by emanations, or aeons (we would say, angels). Thus, Christ gives the Christian what no cult can—namely, fullness. If Christ is Fullness of Life— and the Christian possesses Christ—then the Christian has fullness of life.

How did this completeness, or "fullness" of 2:9, 10, come? It came by

1. The circumcision of Christ (2:11—13a), and
2. The conquest of Christ's cross in canceling sin (2:13b-15).

B. This Life-Style Is Not Regulated by Ascetic Regulations (2:16—3:4).
   1. The Cultists' Approach (2:16—23). Three cardinal features characterized the complexion of the Colossian cult. It received its most detailed development in 2:16-23. Those three traits are:
      a. Jewish-sounding features, involving foods and festivals (2:16, 17);
      b. mystical-sounding features, involving "the worship of angels" (2:18, 19);
      c. ascetic-sounding features (2:20-23), involving "harsh treatment of the body" (2:20-23). The R.S.V. indicates they were "taking . . . [a] stand on visions."
   It is intriguing to compare the Colossian cultists' detailed "dont's" (2:21) with commands found in the *Manual of Discipline* used by the monklike community of Qumran on the Dead Sea shores. Their manual read: "He shall not touch . . . he shall not taste." Probably Paul preserves the actual wording of the cultists slogans.

   Such cults think they are really being more spiritual when actually they have "unspiritual minds" (2:18). Ralph Martin commented on "puffs up," in 2:18, that the cultists were "boasting of their . . . 'fullness' . . . and being full of . . . *gnosis*, when all that they are 'full of' is their pride!"[7]
   2. The Christian Approach (3:1-4).

   "Since you died with Christ" (2:20)
   parallels
   "Since . . . you have been raised with Christ" (3:1).

   In contrast to the cultists' restricting regulations, Christians are raised to a new life. In fact, "Christ . . . is your life" (3:4).

C. This Life-Style Is Characterized by Heaven-on-Earth Character (3:5-17). Christians are not to put down the body, but are to "put to death" the sinful actions that are expressed through the body (3:5). They are to put off five sexual sins (3:5) and five temper-and-tongue sins (3:8). Christians must "put on" the character clothing of the five virtues in 3:12.

D. This Life-Style Is Practiced in Down-to-Earth Relationships (3:18—4:1).

1. Wives and husbands (3:18, 19)
2. Parent and children (3:20. 21)
3. Slaves and masters (3:22—4:1) The section on slaves is noticeably longer, undoubtedly because of the bearing of Onesimus (4:9) on the Colossian church (see Philemon).
   E. This Life-Style Is Supported by Prayerful Wisdom (4:2-6). Paul's prayer encourages Christians in an anti-gnostic setting "so that we may proclaim the *mystery* of Christ" (4:3). And— speaking of *fullness*—instead of being full of pride ("his unspiritual mind puffs him up," 2:18), Paul wants every Christian to be "*full* of grace . . . so that you may know how to answer everyone" (4:6; cp. 1:6, 23, 28).

IV. *Closing Greetings and Grace (4:7-18)*.
   A. Two Letter Carriers (4;7-9)—Tychichus and Onesimus. Onesimus is probably the reason for amplifying the section on slaves (3:22-25). He is the subject of Philemon (chapters 11 and 12 of the study guide).
   B. Three Jewish Stalwarts (4:10, 11)—Aristarchus, Mark, and Jesus Justus. "These are the only Jews among my fellow workers for the kingdom of God" (4:11), leading to the conclusion that Luke (4:14) must be a non-Jew.
   C. Three Gentile Co-Workers (4:12-14)— Epaphras, Luke, and Demas. The probable founder of the Colossian church, Epaphras (1:7, 8), is mentioned here. Like Paul, Epaphras agonized for the Colossians "that you may stand firm in all the will of God, mature and fully assured" (4:12).
   D. Two Local Christians (4:15-18)—Nympha and Archippus. As Paul remembers his chains, he also remembers "grace" (4:18) that can stand sentinel against the encroachments of any cult that would exalt "human tradition" (2:8) and "human commands and teachings" (2:22) rather than the sheer grace of God.

CHAPTER
10

DOCTRINES DEVELOPED IN COLOSSIANS

Imagine side by side a pencil sketch and full-color painting (say a silverpoint or charcoal sketch of Leonardo da Vinci as over against a colorful painting of the same scene by him). Let's assume here that the first drawing is simply a forerunner of the final painted product. Are they the same essential picture? Yes, but the first is sketchier as compared with its fuller, final form.

That illustration is something like what happens in the Bible. God revealed truth progressively. The simpler, sketchier elements generally preceded the fuller form of His revealed truth.

To stretch our analogy some more, let's suppose that we have the seed form of revelation in the Pentateuch (or first five books of Moses), the tender green shoot in the Old Testament Prophets, the blossomed flower in the life of Christ, and the ripened-fruit stage of the plant in Paul's letters. God's revealing of truth is something like the various stages of such a plant.

In Scripture study this type of thinking falls under the heading of Biblical Theology. Biblical Theology studies revealed truth in the various congealed stages of its development at any given point. It does not bulldoze over the different levels of revealed truth in Moses, Amos, Paul, or John. It may even study the historical development of truth as it is presented chronologically at different stages within the various writings of one writer, say, Paul.

Before we distinguish between Systematic Theology and Biblical theology, we must first understand the term *theology*. Some Christians naively say, "Oh, I just want to know the Bible, not Theology" (as if one came from God and the other from humans). However, *both* verse-by-verse Bible study and theology are always colored to some extent by the lenses through which we look. That is why a Presbyterian and Methodist, a Protestant and Mormon can study the same Scripture texts but arrive at different conclusions. One of them, so to speak, has blue-tinted lenses and the other has red-tinted lenses—even though they are looking at the same object.

As used here, *theology* just means "doctrine" or organized teaching of important Bible subjects (e.g., the doctrine of Christ or of salvation). Theology is the study of certain Biblical themes or topics.

Seminaries offer courses in Systematic Theology and Biblical Theology. However, we should not think of Systematic Theology as unbiblical or Biblical Theology as unsystematic. So then, what are these two subjects? Systematic Theology treats the truth of a given theme in the Bible (for example, on the Holy Spirit) without major reference to what Biblical author or stage of history the particular teaching comes from. For instance, the clear theological truth that there is one God goes at least as far back as Deuteronomy 6:4. By gathering up all the information on the theme of God in the Bible, we could organize a doctrine (or Systematic Theology) of God. Systematic Theology is very logical, while Biblical Theology is consciously chronological as well as logical.

Biblical Theology, however, proceeds on a different organizing procedure from Systematic Theology. It does not simply throw together Bible texts from Moses, the Gospels, and Paul as if they are all flatland. It is concerned with the lay of the land, historically speaking. For instance, at what point in history does the church appear? Or, at what point in history is the church first called the Body of Christ? Does Paul use the illustration of "the body" differently at different stages of his writing? Biblical Theology studies separately the theology of Paul, the theology of Peter, the theology of John, etc. As it climbs the theological mountain toward the top of God's revelation, it looks back to see how its present landing stage is different from earlier footholds and examines where it has come to that point.

BIBLICAL THEOLOGY

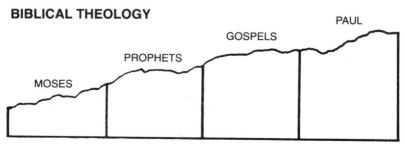

What we are about to do in this chapter is to try to isolate and study what Paul taught about various doctrines within Colossians (in other words, a simplified Biblical Theology of Colossians).

However, before we engage in that project, let's consider the various clusters of letters Paul penned at different time periods. The chart below will help.[1]

FOUR GROUPS OF PAUL'S LETTERS

Letters	Approximate Time	Main Subjects
I and II Thessalonians	A.D. 50-51	Christ's Second Coming
I and II Corinthians Galatians Romans	A.D. 54-57	Sanctification and justification by faith
Philippians, Philemon Colossians, Ephesians	A.D. 60-63	Christ's Person and work, plus Church unity
I Timothy, Titus, II Timothy	A.D. 65-68	Pastoral concerns in the local church

(Note that the Bible books in the left column are given in the general order that orthodox scholars believe Paul wrote them.)

COLOSSIANS' DOCTRINES

God

Colossians' presentation of the doctrine of "God our Father" (1:2) as "the Father of our Lord Jesus Christ" (1:3) is not particularly emphasized or distinguishable from the truth about God the Father in other Pauline writings. Yet God's attributes do not particularly jump out at us in Colossians. God is a grace-and-peace Giver (1:2). God (in contrast to Gnosticism) provides authentic "knowledge" (1:9) and so we can know about God (1:10). This is knowledge of "the invisible God" (1:15). "God has chosen to make known" (1:27) "the mystery of God, namely, Christ" (2:2).

God has a will. Paul's commissioned apostleship stemmed from "the will of God" (1:1). Paul could ask God "to fill you with the knowledge of his will" (1:9), and Epaphras prayed that the Colossian Christians might "stand firm in all the will of God" (4:12).

God's revealing of His secrets is referred to in the phrases:
  (1) "the word of God in its fullness" (1:25)—as over against any gnostic claims of "fullness";
  (2) "the mystery . . . is now disclosed" (1:26);
  (3) "God has chosen to make known . . . this mystery" (1:27; cf. 4:3);
  (4) "the mystery of God" (2:2).

Creation

In contrast to any gnostic views of Creation (of an impure world linked to a pure God through a long, ladderlike line of extended emanations or angels), Paul presented one of the most breathtaking views of Christ and Creation in any of his letters at Colossians 1:15-17. All things stand created from their outset *by* Christ and all things cohere (or hold together) constantly *in* Christ.

Angels

First, observe some *possible* references in Colossians to angels— whether holy or hostile:
  1:16 "thrones or powers or rulers or authorities" (cp. Eph. 6:12);
  2:8 "the elemental spirits of the universe" (NEB);
  2:10 "every power and authority";
  2:15 "the powers and authorities";
  2:18 "the worship of angels";
  2:20 "the elemental spirits of the universe" (NEB).

One of the objectionable Colossian cult features becomes crystallized in Colossians 2:18—angelolatry, or "the worship of angels." Gnosticism interposed a series of emanations, or "elemental spirits of the universe," between God and our world. Thus, these angelic forces functioned as go-betweens between God and humanity and became the "custodians of human destiny."[2]

It is obvious from Colossians 2:15 that some angelic beings in Colossians are viewed as hostile to Christ (cp. Eph. 6:12). Christ conquered them by his cross "to reconcile to himself all things" (1:20). No angels are worthy of worship, for they are created (1:16) and Christ is "over all creation" (1:15). He is "the head over every [angelic] power and authority" (2:10). In fact, in Hebrews 1:6 "all God's angels worship him" (Christ).

Christ

Why is Christ called "the firstborn" (1:15)? Does that mean that

Christ is a created being, as Jehovah's Witnesses hold? (This is a doctrine called Arianism, condemned in the ancient church.) Passages such as John 1:1-3; 5:18; Colossians 2:9; Titus 2:13; Hebrews 1:6, 8; and Revelation 19:10 rule out this possibility.

What then does the title mean? It has a Hebrew heritage. In the Old Testament the firstborn son was normally the chief heir in the household. He held highest honors. The "firstborn" (Hebrew, *bekor*) inherited the "birthright" (*bekorah*).

A comparison of "firstborn" in Colossians 1:15 and "heir" in Hebrews 1:2 reveals that the two titles fall within the same field of ideas, and so they are to be taken as equivalents.

COLOSSIANS 1	HEBREWS 1
1:15 "the image of the invisible"	1:3 "the exact representation of his being"
1:16 "by him all things were created"	1:2 "through whom he made the universe"
1:17 "in him all things hold together"	1:3 "sustaining all things by his powerful word"
1:20 "making peace through his blood"	1:3 "provided purification for sins"

Both Colossians and Hebrews are proving that Christ is "superior to the angels" (Heb. 1:4). Consequently, if all the expressions charted above are basically the same, it stands to reason that the "firstborn over all creation" (Col. 1:15) is equivalent to the "heir of all things" (Heb. 1:2).

Where there is an "inheritance" (Col. 1:12), there must be an heir. Therefore, Christ is the first-ranked Heir, who shares His inheritance with "those who are made holy . . . of the same family" (Heb. 2:11).

This understanding of Christ is harmonious with the awe-inspiring portrayal of Him in Colossians 1:16, 17. Four weighty prepositions are loaded with rich content, as is indicated below:

1. "BY him all things were created" (1:16). Thus, from New Testament revelaton we discover that Christ is the chief agent in Creation and the architect of the ages (Jn. 1:3; I Cor. 8:6; Heb. 1:2). The universe came from the divine Carpenter.
2. "All things were created . . . FOR him" (1:16). Thus, Christ is the goal of history (Heb. 1:2).
3. "He is BEFORE all things" (1:17). This implies Christ's priority to and primacy over Creation. What a breathtaking

affirmation! A man who had already lived and died in Palestine—Paul says He existed before Creation!

4. "IN him all things hold together" (1:17). He is, one might say, God's glue for our globe. Behind the law of centripetal force stands the Son of God. The universe, says Hebrews 1:3, is upheld by His very utterance.

Another one of the most strategic verses in the New Testament bearing upon the true nature of Christ is Colossians 2:9—"For in Christ all the fullness of the Deity lives in bodily form" (cf. 1:19).

Among orthodox Bible commentators there are a number of possible ways to understand Colossians 2:9. However, only two will merit our attention here. It depends upon whether we translate the last expression "in bodily form" (NIV—the corporeal view) or "embodied" (NEB—the corporate view).

Evidently the second option is held by F. F. Bruce and William Hendriksen. They hold that Paul is not referring here to the Incarnation (as Jn. 1:14 or I Tim. 3:16 does). Bruce holds that the Greek word "does not refer to the incarnation as such, but to Christ's complete embodiment" of the "fullness of the Deity," "as contrasted with its supposed distribution through other intermediaries."[3] In other words, instead of God's fullness being embodied in a stairstep series of emanations or "elemental spirits" (as gnostics held), God's fullness is embodied in Christ. William Hendriksen appears to subscribe to this view when he says that "the entire essence and glory of God *is concentrated in Christ as in a body* [or grouping of attributes]. It is in this sense that it can be said that this fullness of the godhead is *embodied, given concrete expression, fully realized, in him.*"[4] This understanding jibes with the type of cult being combatted at Colosse.

By contrast, the more long-standing interpretation of Colossians 2:9 (and the one adopted by most Bible translations) is that "in bodily form" is referring to Christ's incarnation. It is another way of saying "the Word became flesh" (Jn. 1:14). Charles Wesley crystallized this exalted view of Christ in our Christmas carol:

> Veiled in flesh, the Godhead see;
> Hail th' Incarnate deity!
> Pleased as man with men to dwell.
> Jesus our Emmanuel!

Colossians 1:15-20 and 2:3 and 9 provide us with some of the most elevated passages on the person of Christ. Colossians also comments on the work of Christ. Colossians 1:20 speaks of "his blood, shed on the cross," and 1:22 of "Christ's physical body [going] through death." Christ's cross (2:15) became the vehicle of His conquest over hostile angelic authorities; although, Paul nowhere explains what this specifically entails.

We will consider several of the benefits of Christ's cross-work (namely, redemption and forgiveness, 1:14; and peace, 1:20) under the heading of Salvation.

As he does in his other epistles, Paul asserts that "God . . . raised him [Christ] from the dead" (2:12). Now "Christ is seated at the right hand of God" (3:1).

The Spirit

Interestingly, almost no mention is made of the Holy Spirit in Colossians. Perhaps this is because the cultists claimed mystical, supernatural experiences (cf. 2:18). As a result, Paul's only explicit reference to the Holy Spirit is to the Colossian Christians' "love in the Spirit" (1:8). By paralleling Colossians 3:16 with Ephesians 5:18, 19, we may assume that the "spiritual songs" were spawned by the Spirit of God.

Sin

Colossians is not overly endowed with information about sinful human nature. Undoubtedly, this is because Paul's arrow was aimed at the more sophisticated and disguised form of sin in the form of the Colossian cult. Nevertheless, Colossians 1:21 affirms that prior to becoming Christians, the Colossians "were alienated from God and were enemies in your mind." Paul writes that "you were dead in your sins and in the uncircumcision of your sinful nature" (2:13; cp. Eph. 2:1-3, 11, 12).

Their "sinful nature" (2:13) flowered in the poisonous form of various "sins" (2:13). In Colossians 3:5 and 8 Paul listed two sets of five sins. He calls these collectively "whatever belongs to your earthly nature" (3:5) and "the life you once lived" (3:6). Indeed, these constitute the "old self with its practices" (3:9). Unlike the gnostic-type cults, Paul does not blame these practices merely on the body, for in 1:21 he pinpoints the source of enmity as "the mind." Paul presented a cause-and-effect relationship between those sins and "the wrath of God" (3:6).

Salvation

If the previous heading represents our "Before" picture, this heading surveys our "After" condition—and what God and Christ have done to bring this about. Before a more detailed look, survey the key expressions charted below.

qualified (1:12)
share in the inheritance (1:12)
in the kingdom (1:12)
rescued us (1:13)
brought us into the kingdom (1:13)
we have redemption (1:14)
the forgiveness of sins (1:14; cf. 2:13; 3:13)
making peace through his blood (1:20)
reconciled you (1:22)
you received Christ (2:6)
you have been given fullness in Christ (2:10)
you were . . . circumcised, in the putting off of the sinful nature (2:11)
having been buried with him in baptism (2:12)
raised with him through your faith (2:12; cp. 3:1)
made . . . alive with Christ (2:13)
canceled the written code . . . that was against us (2:14)
died with Christ (2:20; 3:3)
hidden with Christ (3:3)
you have taken off your old self (3:9)
you . . . have put on the new self (3:10)

Given the size of this epistle, this is one of Paul's richest, being pimentoed with expressions about what Christ has done for and in the Christian in salvation. Colossians' twin epistle, Ephesians (especially chapter 2), can be compared for similarity. In fact, it seems quite reasonable to hold that Paul wrote Ephesians as a circular letter for churches on the same general subjects, but without the same specificity of the local cult threat as in Colossians.

The saving acts in Colossians 1:12 and 13 are attributed "to the Father," while it is "the Son . . . in whom we have redemption," explained as "the forgiveness of sins" (1:14).

To be redeemed, forgiven (1:14), and reconciled (1:22) are all pictorial ramps into the same stadium of salvation. "Redemption" (1:14) views us as slaves in sin's slave market who have been bought with a ransom payment. "Forgiveness" (1:14) subtracts the sum total of sins on our ledger and removes them. "Reconciled" (1:22) makes us other than we once were, i.e., "alienated . . . and . . . enemies" (1:21). Paul would surely agree with Hebrews 2:3 that ours is "such a great salvation"!

 What pictures from modern life might you use to express what Christ has done for you and in you?

Paul "disinfected" (to use H. Chadwick's term) several of the cult's slogan-words to explain salvation to the Colossian Christians. He wanted them to *"know* the *mystery* of God, namely, Christ" (2:6). They had *"received* Christ" (2:6). The Greek word for "received" was a technical term for handing down tradition (such as gnostic cultists would do; 2:8, 22). In contrast to gnostics, Christians "have been given *fullness* in Christ" (2:10). Fulfillment is found in the One who is fullness of life.

As Paul does in Ephesians (2:5, 6), he emphasizes the "with" phase of a Christian's unitedness and togetherness with Christ. In salvation Christians are:

(1) "buried with him" (2:12; cf. 2:20);
(2) "raised with him" (2:12);
(3) "made alive with Christ" (2:13);
(4) "raised with Christ" (3:1);
(5) "hidden with Christ" (3:3).

They are coexperiencers of all that Christ has undergone. They are united "with" Christ because they are "in Christ" (2:9; Eph. 1:3; 2:6, 13).

Another aspect of salvation is treated under the categories of the "old self" and "new self" (3:9, 10 paralleled in Eph. 4:22-24). The "old self" is explicitly referred to in three New Testament verses—Romans 6:6; Ephesians 4:22; and Colossians 3:9. The "old self" is the sinning, unchristian person, enslaved to his former ways. The expression is translated "old nature" in the R.S.V. The "new self," or "new nature," is the new person who is in Christ. In Colossians the taking off of the old self is viewed as past (3:9—at conversion).

Christian Experience

A new life-style is imperative for a new self or nature. The bulk of Colossians 2:6—4:6 maps out a number of phases in the Christian life-style. Instead of a false "fullness" and "knowledge" (*gnosis*), the Christian experience comes from being *"fill*[ed] . . . with the knowledge of his [God's] will" (1:10). Paul urges an *epignosis* (the Greek word in 1:9, 10 might be translated "thorough knowledge"). This life blossoms in faith, faithfulness, and love (1:2, 4, 8; 2:2, 5; 3:14).

The deeper spiritual experience (if we may imagine the Colossian cult using such terminology) is no unfluttered, conflict-exempt life. Paul, as model, wrote: "I want you to know how much I am stuggling"

(2:1). Epaphras was "always wrestling" for the Colossian church in prayer (4:13).

The Christian life is one for sin-vigilantes who "put to death" particular sins in themselves (3:5, 8). They clothe themselves in the character clothing of Christ (3:12-14). The "peace of Christ" (3:15) and "the word of Christ" (3:16) are to steer them "as members of one body" (3:15).

The Christian life is no life on a higher plane—if by "a higher plane" we mean one that weasels out of marriage adjustments, changing dirty diapers, and avoiding labor-management disputes. Colossians 3:18—4:1 makes it clear that the one whose heart and mind are "set . . . on things above" (3:1) must maintain responsible, respectful relationships in marriage, family, and employment settings. All racial, education, social, and economic levels demand respect (3:11).

"The way you act toward outsiders" (4:5) involves prayer and proclamation, wisdom and winsomeness (4:2-6). In contrast to gnostic, or cult thinking, Christianity is marketed and targeted for "everyone" (1:28; 4:6), not merely for some spiritual aristocracy.

The Church

While most other doctrines in Ephesians and Colosians find considerable overlap—or at least some parallel—with doctrines in Paul's other epistles, his doctrine of the church in Ephesians and Colossians has a more distinctive development.

Paul depicts the Church as the Body of Christ. He used the picture of the body in Romans, I Corinthians, Ephesians, and Colossians. However, he used the body illustration somewhat differently in the two earlier epistles (Romans and I Corinthians) than he did in the two later companion epistles (Ephesians and Colossians).

First, study the chart on the next page to get a basic idea of the different emphases.

TIME OF WRITING	EPISTLES	EMPHASES
A.D. 54-57	I Corinthians 12 Romans 12	Christ's body has many members with varying gifts
A.D. 60-63	Ephesians Colossians	Christ is the head of the body, the Church

Read Romans 12:4, 5 and I Corinthians 12:12-27. Note that both of these earlier Pauline epistles couch the body illustration in the context of spiritual gifts Christians possess (Rom. 12:6-8; I Cor. 12:4-11, 28-30). Just as all the parts of a physical body have a valuable function to perform within the unity of that body, even so all Christians have spiritual gifts to use for the benefit of the church.

 Does the average church today take seriously the idea that every Christian has some spiritual gift to use within the context of the church? Do you know what your spiritual gift is?

With regard to Christ's headship, William Hendriksen stated: "In the writings of Paul this expression is something new. . . . It is nowhere found in the earlier epistles such as Galatians, I and II Thessalonians, I and II Corinthians, or Romans."[5] Study its usage in Ephesians 1:22, 23; 2:16; 4:12, 16; 5:29, 30; and Colossians 1:18, 24; and 2:19.

End Times

Theologians speak about eschatology (meaning, a study of the end times). They also speak about realized and future eschatology. This is the difference between the "already" and "not yet" aspects of God's Kingdom. In other words, God's Kingdom can be spoken of as both present ("already") and future ("not yet"). These two phases of the Kingdom of God run throughout the New Testament. For the present aspect of that Kingdom, see Luke 11:20; for the future aspect, see Matthew 25:31 and 34.

Colossians has three references to "the Kingdom" ("the kingdom of light," 1:12; "the kingdom of the Son he loves," 1:13; and "the kingdom of God," 4:11). (The word "Kingdom" is not actually found in the original Greek text of 1:12.) At least the last two references seem to refer to the Kingdom in its present phase. Over 1900 years ago the Colossian Christians had already been "brought . . . into the kingdom" (1:13).

There is only one explicit reference in Colossians to Christ's Second Coming. It is Colossians 3:4 ("when Christ . . . appears"). Christian slaves could be assured that "you also will appear with him in glory" (3:4) and "you will receive an inheritance from the Lord" (3:24), your "Master in heaven" (4:1). This is part of "the hope that is stored up for you in heaven" (1:5).

11

HANDLE WITH CARE
Philemon 1-10

? How many scenes can you think of from plays, literature, or real life that occurred in prisons? Can you think of any good results that came out of those prison experiences?

Charles Dickens's *Oliver Twist* begins in debtor's prison with the death of the boy's mother. Also Dickens's *Tale of Two Cities* revolves around the prison experiences of Dr. Manet and Charles Darnay in France during the revolution. Rip-roaring adventure stories like Victor Hugo's *Les Miserables* and Alexandre Dumas's *Man in the Iron Mask* and *The Count of Monte Cristo* are set in a backdrop of prison experience.

John Bunyan, the Bedford [England] tinker, penned his classic *The Pilgrim's Progress* during his intermittent 12-year period of imprisonment. Franz Kafka's *The Trial* and Bernard Malamud's *The Fixer* revolve around prison situations.

Many of the great masterpieces of Russian literature were forged in, or revolve around, the prison experience. A girl in prison is featured in Leo Tolstoy's *The Resurrection*. Fyodr Dostoevsky, who spent some years in a Siberian labor camp and six years of forced service in the army, gave the world *Crime and Punishment*. More recently, Alexander Solzhenitsyn, Nobel prizewinner, experienced such persecution. *One Day in the Life of Ivan Denisovich* by Solzhenitsyn reveals the inhumane hardships of incarceration in a labor camp. Modern stories set against prison backdrops include *Papillon*, *White Knights*, and *Runaway Train*.

Many admirable persons have suffered in prison cells and camps—some as victors over brutality; others as victims in death. Corrie ten Boom, Dietrich Bonhoeffer, Watchman Nee—time would fail us were we to recite the litany of names on the list of prison nobility. Indeed, "the world was not worthy of them" (Heb. 11:38).

Richard Lovelace said: "Stone walls do not a prison make nor iron bars a cage." Prison is never a pretty place. Yet "Samuel Rutherford headed his letters from prison, 'Christ's Palace, Aberdeen,' and declared that every stone in the wall shone like a ruby."[1] Obviously, his perspective transformed prison.

The more one contemplates this theme, the more impressive the list of "prison epistles" becomes (Ephesians, Philippians, Colossians, and Philemon).

Philemon traditionally is thought to have been written in Rome where Paul was held prisoner in his own rented house (Acts 28, though Ephesus and Caesarea have also been suggested). If Paul was held in Rome, Onesimus must have fled a thousand miles to get away.

E. M. Blaiklock has suggested imaginatively, "Perhaps the simple boy from the Lycus valley [Onesimus, oh-NESS-ih-mus] was no match for the slum-dwellers by the Tiber [in Rome]. Robbed, . . . perhaps sick in that notoriously malarial environment, beaten by the alien horde, Onesimus may have been recognized by the good Epaphras [Philem. 23; Col. 4:12] from Colossae."[2]

Before Paul wrote to Philemon about A.D. 60-63, Onesimus had evidently been converted (Philem. 10, 11) through Paul. Paul sent Onesimus back (Col. 4:9) evidently as one of those carrying the Letters to the Colossians and Philemon. This study spotlights this reunion of slave and owner.

TRUE OR FALSE

_____ 1. The Bible says that Onesimus stole some money from his slave owner Philemon.

_____ 2. The Bible says that Onesimus met Paul in Rome.

_____ 3. The Bible says that Paul is a type of Christ who was willing to pay our debt.

Did you put a "T" by any of the above three questions? If so, mark them wrong. They are intended as trick questions, because these sort of statements are often passed on as if they are Biblical facts. Closer reading, however, will show you that none of them are actual Biblical statements. The first two are legitimately possible interpretations, but none of the three are strict facts of Scripture.

Here is a short summary of Philemon:

I.   Greetings (Saying "Hi")—1-3
II. Gratitude (Saying "Thanks")—4-7
III. Appeal (Speaking softly)—8-22
IV. Addendum (Saying "So long")—23-25

INTRODUCTION

The Epistle to Philemon is the shortest of all Paul's surviving writings—335 words in the Greek text. While the Epistles to Timothy and Titus are also addressed to individuals, they contain additional church-laden overtones. The Epistle to Philemon is Paul's most private, personal, revealing, polite letter among the New Testament writings. Colossians and Philemon were most likely written at the same time. Seven out of the ten names in Colossians 4:7-17 are found in Philemon (2, 10, 23, and 24). Onesimus is said to be "one of you" Colossian Christians (Col. 4:9). Thus, it is most appropriate that we study Philemon side by side with Colossians.

I. Saying 'Hi' (1-3)

Like all of Paul's stereotyped salutations, the apostle uses the skeletal structure that answers:

    (1) Who? ("Paul . . . and Timothy");

    (2) To whom? ("To Philemon," etc.);

    (3) What? ("Grace . . . and peace").

Notice all the telltale mementoes of a prisoner in Ephesians 3:1; 4:1; 6:20; Philippians 1:7, 13, 17; 4:22; Colossians 4:3, 10, 18; and Philemon 1. George Buttrick commented aptly: "Mark carefully that he does not say 'prisoner of the Romans.' They made the arrest, and the Jews brought the charges; but both groups, together with the jailer, were only small-part actors in the drama,"[3] for Paul is "a prisoner of Jesus Christ" (vs. 1). Can we write, "employee of Jesus Christ," "housewife for Jesus Christ," "tennis player of Jesus Christ"?

 How can Paul's perspective on prison alter our attitude toward adverse circumstances?

 Have you ever been in a Paul-Timothy sort of Christian relationship? What are the ingredients necessary to maintain such a relationship?

Practically all that we know of the recipient of this letter is what we can garner from the confines of this book. Just as the Colossian Epaphras was "dear" (Col. 1:7), and Paul's travelling companion (Luke) was "dear" (Col. 4:14), so also Philemon was a "dear" friend to Paul (Philem. 1). Interestingly, Paul uses the same descriptive word for slave and (presumed) slave owner—"dear," or beloved. Philemon, Paul's "dear friend" (vs. 1), is asked to accept back Onesimus "as a dear brother" (vs. 16). Note that Philemon is not explicitly called Onesimus's slave master, although that is the traditional assumption most reasonably concluded from the text.

Paul influenced many noble women on his travels (Acts 16:14, 15; 17:12; 18:2, 26). Among these women was Apphia, assumed to be the wife of Philemon (vs. 2). Scholars have uncovered an inscription about another Apphia at Colosse that reads:

HERMAS IN MEMORY OF APPHIA, HIS BELOVED WIFE, DAUGHTER OF TRYPHON, A COLOSSIAN BY BIRTH.

Along with Apphia, Archippus is addressed (vs. 2) and calls upon him to "complete the work you have received in the Lord" (Col. 4:17). Edward Lohse observed, "Both in Philemon and in Colossians, Archippus and Onesimus are mentioned outside the list of greetings proper [Col. 4:10-15; Philem. 23, 24]."[4]

In verse 2 the "your" is singular in Greek, and it is assumed that the church group meets in Philemon's home.

 Early Christian churches met in an assortment of buildings. At least one Jerusalem group met in "the house of Mary the mother of John, also called Mark" (Acts 12:12). For two years Paul "had discussions daily in the lecture hall of Tyrannus" in Ephesus (Acts 19:9). At Troas Paul talked until midnight in an "upstairs room" (Acts 20:8).

Henry Sefton stated, "The earliest church [building] of which traces remain is a normal Syrian courtyard house which has been adapted for the purpose. Two rooms were put together for the celebration of the Lord's Supper, another room served as the place for baptisms."[5] At Dura-Europus, on the Euphrates River, the adapted room might hold a hundred people. "The house had been built A.D. 232-233."[6]

 What advantages and disadvantages would there be to a house church?

The first part of Philemon 3 is exactly the same as Colossians 1:2—presumably carried to the same city at the same time. "Grace" (vs. 3)—in the form of graciousness—would be a much-needed quality by

Philemon in order to carry out Paul's request. "Peace" (vs. 3)—in the form of harmony—could be the outcome of a resolution to the problem at hand.

II. Saying Thanks (4-7)

John Knox aptly commented, "The 'thanksgiving' [vss. 4-6 or 4-7 in Philemon] in Paul's letters has a character somewhat analogous to that of the overture of an opera—the themes to be elaborated in the body of the epistle are briefly struck [here]."[7]

THE WORD	THE OVERTURE	THE ELABORATION
prayers	vs. 4	vs. 22
love	vs. 5	vss. 7, 9
sharing	vs. 6	vs. 17 partners (same in Greek)
good	vs. 6	vs. 14 in Greek
brother	vs. 7	vs. 20
refreshed	vs. 7	vs. 20
hearts	vs. 7	vss. 12, 20

The thanksgiving section of Philemon, vss. 4-6, is the shortest of all those in Paul's writings—47 words.

Philemon was a microcosm—a mini-version—of the Colossian church. We discover this by matching the remnant of cloth in Philemon 4 with the bolt of material in Colossians 1:4. What is true of the Colossian church in general (love and loyalty) is true of Philemon in particular.

 What do you think are the three outstanding characteristics of your local church? How do you match up with those three characteristics?

 It may be that we have an example of *chiasm* (KAI-az-uhm) in verse 4. *Chiasm* comes from the Greek letter *chi (kai)*, which looks like a large X in English. Just as the letter *chi* has crossing arms, so some sentences have a crossing pattern. In this pattern the first and fourth items match, and the second and third items match, forming an A B B A structure.

The chiasm can be seen by considering the King James Version of verse 4 (which preserves the Greek word order) "love and faith, which thou hast toward the Lord Jesus and toward all the saints." Do "love and faith" go equally with both the Lord Jesus and the saints, or which goes with which? It seems most natural (as the NIV assumes) to relate "faith" to the Lord Jesus and "love" to the saints. Thus, the first and fourth items pair off, and the second and third items form a couple. This can be seen in the diagram on the next page:

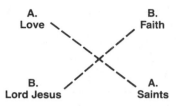

The crossing (or *chi*-shaped) pattern forms a literary chiasm.

Not only that, but by comparing verse 4 with verses 5 and 6 we see another chiasm.

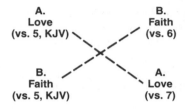

? Can you think of some concrete ways you have seen faith and love displayed in other Christians?

Verse 6 is most obscure. Some of this obscurity is due to the fact that the term "communication" (KJV) or "sharing" (NIV) may be understood or translated in different ways.

Ω The Greek word *koinonia* (*koy-know-NEE-uh*) is one of those few words that Christians who have never studied Greek sometimes like to use. *Koine* (*koy-NAY*) Greek is the common language of the New Testament, spoken generally by the common people. *Koinos* meant "common." James and John were *koinonoi* (plural) with Simon in the fishing business (Lk. 5:10). They were partners, sharing fishing in common (cf. II Cor. 6:14).

In different contexts *koinonia* can take on different flavorings. Some of its meanings are:
 (1) a mystical meaning—"communion" (I Cor. 10:20);
 (2) a social meaning—"fellowship" (Acts 2:42);
 (3) a financial meaning—"contribution" (Rom. 15:26);
 (4) a communicational meaning—"communication" (in the modern sense).

Which meaning is meant in Philemon 6? This is where you see how differently various Bible translators have understood this expression. The second meaning is adopted by the Good News Bible: "our fellowship with you as believers." The fourth (evangelistic) meaning is adopted by the Living Bible ("as you share your faith with others it will grip their lives too").

Similarly, "faith" has two possible interpretations: (1) your inward believing (subjective); (2) the basic body of beliefs (objective)—"our common faith" (NEB).

 What relationship do you see between the two meanings of faith above?

 The Greek word translated "active" in verse 6 is found in the New Testament three times (I Cor. 16:9; Heb. 4:12; Philem. 6). A slightly different form of the Greek term is used "of a mill in working order."[8] Every Christian ought to be in good working order (like a Boeing 707 ready for takeoff) when it comes to communicating with other Christians and non-Christians.

 In what way might you become a "joygiving" (to borrow P. T. O'Brien's term) to others?

Twice within this letter (almost a long memo) Paul used the expression "refresh my bowels" (KJV; vss. 7 and 20). The word translated "bowels" in the King James Version is difficult to translate. It does not refer to the lower intestines, but to the *viscera* (i.e., the heart, lungs, liver, etc.). The Greeks selected this bodily area as the source of emotions, the innermost feelings. When English-speaking people say, "It touched my heart," they aren't actually referring to the physical pump organ, but to their sense of compassion. Paul spoke similarly here.

Some have thought that Paul may have been referring to Philemon's possible financial generosity—if the letter is coming after the earthquake in that same region in A.D. 60.

III. Speaking Softly (8-22)
A. Prisoner Becomes Persuader (8-10)

In these three verses we can almost crawl inside the skullcap of Paul and observe the thoughts ticking away in his head ("I could . . . order," vs. 8; "Yet I appeal," vs. 9; "I appeal," vs. 10). There is a battle raging inside his brain. On one side of the battlefield was entrenched his artillery as an apostle. Apostles could command like great army generals (cf. I Cor. 7:10; I Thess. 4:11). However, rather than acting as a commanding general, Paul did not pull rank on Philemon.

Paul's letter to Philemon is a masterpiece in love's art of persuasion. First, Paul urged Philemon to do "what you ought to do" (vs. 8). This

Stoic phrase, found only elsewhere in the New Testament at Ephesians 5:4 and Colossians 3:18, refers to whatever is one's proper duty. Paul functions here almost as a spiritual counterpart to an Emily Post or Amy Vanderbilt. There is a spiritual etiquette built into Christian love. Even Long John Silver the pirate in *Treasure Island* liked to repeat, "Duty is duty."

Instead of candidly commanding Philemon's conduct, Paul appealed "on the basis of love" (vs. 9). This second appeal should have struck a resounding chord within Philemon, for Paul had already complimented him for his love in verses 5 and 7.

Third, Paul removed the matter from the realm of "have to." Twice he asked (vss. 9, 10) rather than barking orders like a drill sergeant. (Which approach do you find more appealing from someone higher up—an order or a request?)

Fourth, the one appealing is "aged" (vs. 9). At the stoning of Stephen, Paul was a young man (Acts 7:58). The ancient doctor Hippocrates (for whom the modern Hippocratic oath is named) divided a man's life into seven stages. The sixth of Hippocrates's seven life stages was from 49 to 56 years old. The word for "aged" in verse 9 is the same as Hippocrates's sixth age level. Probably Paul was between 50 and 60 years old when he wrote to Philemon.

Many commentators take exception here and hold that the Greek word does not mean "aged" but "ambassador." This meaning also makes good sense in light of its use in Ephesians 6:20, which could have been "written perhaps on the same day as this."[9]

Not only is there a twinge of feeling in that the request rises from a gentleman of years, but also it comes from "a prisoner" (vs. 9). Many believe Paul wrote the Prison Epistles of Ephesians (4:1; 6:20); Philippians (1:7, 13, 16); Colossians (4:3, 18); and Philemon (1, 9, 10, 23) about the same time, probably between A.D. 60 and 63 from Rome.

A sixth basis of appeal to Philemon is a transformed Onesimus (vs. 10). Paul called Onesimus "my son," just as he called Timothy (I Tim. 1:2) and Titus (Titus 1:4) by similar titles. Most assume this to mean that Onesimus was born into God's family due to Paul. In the Jewish Babylonian Talmud it is written: "When a man teaches the son of another the Torah [or first five books of the Bible], the Scripture treats him as if he had begotten him."[10]

Something momentous had happened during Paul's incarceration. That something was a young man—a runaway slave—named Onesimus. How did Onesimus wind up with Paul? We don't know. What we do know is that, for Paul, his prison became a spiritual maternity ward. Just as Oliver Twist's mother gave physical birth to her son in debtor's prison, so Paul evidently gave spiritual birth to his "son Onesimus" (vs. 10) in a prison house.

Not only was this runaway slave Paul's spiritual son, but the slave's master, Philemon, apparently owed *his* spiritual life to Paul also (vs. 19). Reuniting a runaway slave with his owner in a brand-new relationship—that was Paul's purpose in writing this extraordinary letter.

The last clause in verse 10 may mean that Onesimus's conversion occurred while he was a jail mate of Paul's. How their paths crossed is not known for sure. If the jail was in Rome (the traditional view), Onesimus must have traveled over a thousand miles from Colosse. One ancient historian had called Rome "the common cesspool of the world." In that case, Onesimus chose to roost with birds of a feather. But the long arm of the law was the means to bring him into grace. Ah, yes, grace—a charming sound!

CHAPTER
12

REWIRING RELATIONSHIPS

Philemon 11-25

Facts and figures on slavery in the Roman Empire vary, but those listed below will provide some index into the prevailing conditions. The slave population of Attica (an area of Greece controlled by Athens) around 430 B.C. was about 115,000 out of a regional population of 315,000, according to Time-Life's *Classical Greece*. There were 120 million people in the Roman empire, with probably half to three-fourths of them slaves. J. W. Shepherd said, "Two thousand lords in Rome had 1,300,000 slaves . . . . In the Empire there were 6,000,000 slaves."[1] George Ladd wrote, "It has been estimated that in the time of Paul there were as many slaves as free men in Rome, and the proportion of slaves to free men has been put as high as three to one."[2]

Onesimus was a Colossian (Col. 4:9) slave (Philem. 16). Colosse was a city in the region of Phrygia. There was a proverb that ran, "A Phrygian [slave] is the better . . . for a beating."[3] In that time slave masters held the power of death over runaway slaves. One friend of the Roman Emperor Augustus even threw slaves into his fish pond to feed his electric eels. In A.D. 61 (around the very time the Letter to Philemon was written) one Roman senator was murdered by his slave. Roman law prescribed that all 400 of his slaves should be killed. By contrast, how different was the treatment Paul proposed for Onesimus!

Have you ever taken on the job of rewiring a house? It would require a good deal of technical expertise plus a bundle of patience. In the Letter to Philemon (and in Christianity) we engage in recircuitry. We are seeking to rewire relationships. As Ralph Martin put it, Paul was seeking to construct a "network of new situations and the circuit of new relations."[4]

THE ODD TRIO

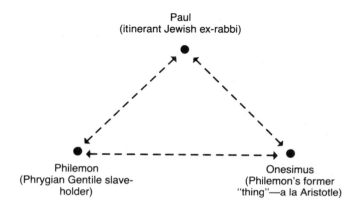

Here we are dealing not merely with the Odd Couple, but the Odd Trio. God deals in unlikely networkings. (Imagine disciple Matthew, the ex-tax collector—and pro-Roman traitor to Jews—going out on a mission two by two with Simon the Zealot, rabid anti-Roman crusader. It might have made for some interesting—and heated—conversations!) In this recircuiting process Paul was attempting to hook up (probably) a runaway renegade slave with his ex-master. (Best of luck, Dale Carnegie!)

Consider the real-life characters in this dramatic plot. Once upon a time Paul had undoubtedly thanked God every morning that God had not made him a slave. Obviously Paul had gotten rewired.

Philemon's previous networking with Onesimus was this:

> "Me-up-here;
> You-down-there."

Philemon, Onesimus's owner, must have been a wealthy merchant since he owned slaves. Perhaps he ran a weaving establishment, for Colosse was famed for its *colossenos*, a reddish-colored dye in Colossian cloth.

However, Paul's electrical wiring had become intermeshed with Philemon's, for verse 19 ("you owe your very self to me," GNB) would seem to imply that Philemon had had Paul as his spiritual midwife.

In the interim, however, Paul had begotten another son—Onesimus. Paul was spiritual parent to both slave owner and slave. Therefore, spiritually Philemon and Onesimus were on the same plane, but socially they were on a different plane. The crucial question of this letter is: how is the spiritual relationship going to bisect this social relationship?

Useless Becomes Useful (11-15)

Frequently slaves possessed names like "Good," "Pleasing," or "Profitable." Paul was not against an occasional play on words. Verse 11 is a good example. The name Onesimus meant "useful." That was probably worth a laugh to Philemon! (What runaway slave could possibly be useful?) But Paul pulled a shocker with the news that the "useless" one "has become useful" (vs. 11). Obviously Onesimus had undergone a Christian conversion and Paul had lab tested this change in life's lab by observing measurable, behavioral changes. As Charles Campbell put it, the slave was returning as an *Onesimus* person.[5] Onesimus's name now jibed with his new nature.

Conversion, however, was not Glamorville for Onesimus. It meant being sent back to the slave owner from whom he had (probably) stolen. Imagine the quavery feelings Onesimus must have felt.

Paul had no legal rights for retaining a runaway slave. Therefore he "sent" (a Greek word containing legal overtones, like our *extradition*) Onesimus back (vs. 12). That very same Greek word for "sent" is used in Luke 23:7, 11, and 15—where Pilate and Herod "sent" Jesus back and forth in a trial setting. In verse 12 Paul called Onesimus "mine own bowels" (KJV). This is the same expression as in verse 7, referring not to one's lower intestines but to the *viscera* (that is, heart, lungs, liver). For Greek people this was considered the center of emotion. Therefore, Paul had become attached to Onesimus by a kind of emotional adhesive tape.

? Has Christianity created any deep emotional attachments in you for other Christians? If you balk at that question, what do you think may be the reasons for your hesitation?

Once more, in verses 13 and 14, Paul is torn with conflicting emotions. On the one hand, he "was preferring" (possible translation of vs. 13) to retain Onesimus. It was desire versus duty. Consequently, his decision (vs. 14) had to compute Philemon's verdict on the subject. Therefore, Paul's will won out over his wishes.

Another persuasive barb is couched inside Paul's statement that he would not override Philemon's persuasion ("without your consent," vs. 14). Consent rather than coercion is always preferable. How different from legalism, which says, "Do as I say, or *else*!" Inasmuch as a runaway slave could be punished by torture or put to death, Philemon had to be consulted (vs. 14). In Rome Onesimus had functioned as one of Paul's ministers (vs. 13). Hence, Paul commended Onesimus's value—more than a slave's market value—to his owner. Yet he wanted Philemon's choice to be free rather than forced (vs. 14).

In order to persuade Philemon, Paul put Onesimus's flight in a new light. He did not say, "That scoundrel ran off." As William Hendriksen put it, "Behold *the hand of God* rather than the guilty hands of Onesimus."[6] In verse 15 Paul reenacts, as it were, the Old Testament experience of Joseph. Joseph had run his "bad" experiences through the gristmill of a providential perspective. As a result he concluded, "You [his brothers] intended to harm me, but God intended it for good" (Gen. 50:20). In retrospect, Joseph had seen God working all things together for good (Rom. 8:28). There is a definite hint of the same providential perspective in verse 15. The verb "departed" in the King James Version (active voice) should be translated "was separated" (passive voice). This implied that God was at work in Onesimus's separation from Philemon. Thus, rather than lambaste Onesimus for his illegal act, Paul places it under the lens of divine providence. Paul demonstrated in vs. 15 that eternal good had emerged from the temporary bad.

? Can you recall an occasion when something that seemed bad turned out for good by God's providence?

Servant Becomes Brother (16-18)

How would you treat some internationally recognized Christian figure, like a Billy Graham, if that person were to walk into your church by surprise one Sunday morning? Would you react the same way if "John Smith," who once stole the morning offering from your church, returned one Sunday carrying a letter written by a neighboring pastor stating John's conversion? If you grasp the connection between those two preceding reactions, then you have felt the air-hammer impact of what Paul was asking in verses 16 and 17.

Many slave masters resorted to cruel torture for misbehaving slaves. Thus, Paul's compliments for Onesimus and his requests to Philemon amount to this: roll out the red carpet for a repentant runaway slave. Paul's suggested treatment was a total turnabout from much of the opinion rife in the Roman Empire.

George Buttrick said of verse 16: "This sentence is in some regards the heart of the epistle."[7] Ralph Martin said, "Paul's statement of verse 16 is the Magna Carta of true emancipation and human dignity."[8]

THE SLAVERY QUESTION

Why doesn't the New Testament insist on the outright abolition of slavery? The closest Paul came to it perhaps is I Corinthians 7:21b. F. W. Beare cautions, "It must be remembered . . . that there was little free labor in the world of that time. . . . The freedman generally became a hanger-on of some wealthy house, as dependent on his patron's bounty as any slave, or sank into the mass of the urban proletariat, eking out a precarious existence on the public dole of grain. The indiscriminate bestowal of freedom was simply not feasible in the social conditions of the time."[9]

 How would you explain the issue of slavery to someone who seems morally indignant and claims that the New Testament sanctions such forms of oppression?

The New Testament does not champion violent, radical social revolution. However, it does plant the seeds of deep spiritual and social respect so as eventually to yield a crop of changed civilization. Such a revolutionary principle eventually broke the backbone of slavery. Someone has said verse 16 is the seed planted inside the rock of slavery that burst it when it grew to full flower. Early reformers, such as William Wilberforce of Great Britain's House of Commons, believed that they were operating from the base of Christian principle in legalizing the emancipation of slaves.

In the play Miss Julie, Jean, the 30-year-old male servant, says to the princess, Miss Julie: "If it's true that a thief can get to heaven and be with the angels, it's pretty strange that a laborer's child here on earth mayn't come in the park and play with the Count's daughter." Miss Julie replies, "Do you think all poor children feel the way you did? . . . It must be terrible to be poor." The countess then expresses her surprise at the educated manner in which Jean has expressed himself. In return, he expresses his surprise at the bad language the upper classes use, saying, "I couldn't think where you had learnt such words. Perhaps, at bottom, there isn't as much difference between people as one's led to believe."[10]

Likewise, in Gustav Flaubert's story *Felicite* a similar scene is enacted. Felicite is the maid servant for whom the story is entitled. The story revolves around her somewhat dismal life of losses—the loss of her fiance while young, the loss of her prized nephew in death, the loss of the aristocratic child under Felicite's care—Virginia, etc. In one touching moment Felicite consoles Virginia's mother who is of a higher social caste than herself. The servant and mistress kiss, and—says Flaubert—the kiss "equalized them for a moment."

In verse 16, that Magna Carta verse, Paul was not formally asking Philemon to free Onesimus from slavery; he was inaugurating a totally *new* treatment: Paul was asking this slave owner to have a personal respect and a partner relationship with his slave. At the social level they remained owner and slave, but at the spiritual level they had become equals.

Seneca, the Roman thinker, had said, "Kindly remember that he whom you call your slave sprang from the same stock, is smiled upon by the same skies, and on equal terms with yourself breathes, lives, and dies."[11] Nevertheless, Seneca's brand of thinking was the rare exception. For instance, Aristotle, the Greek philosopher, had said that "between slave and master there is no proper reciprocity; the master may be a hundred things besides the slave's master, [but] the slave is absolutely nothing but the master's slave."[12]

Verse 16 detonates the long-fused explosive words: "no longer as a slave, but better than a slave, as a dear brother." Here is the recircuitry of relationships. Paul calls not merely for Onesimus's rehabilitation (evidently without any punishment), but for a relationship of respect (from master to slave). Treating someone as an equal in spiritual relationships tends to melt away demeaning social relationships, like slavery.

Paul stresses a slave's worth "both as a man and as a brother in the Lord" (as a human being and as a Christian). In contrast to Aristotle, Paul asserted that Onesimus had worth not merely as a Christian ("as a brother") but also as a person ("as a man"). Therefore, despite the consensus of social thought at that time, Paul affirmed the worth of all humans, irrespective of their social status.

Bartholomew de Las Casas's father had travelled to the West Indies with Columbus on his second major voyage westward. Las Casas underwent a spiritual conversion in the New World. This conversion radically changed his outlook about how the Spaniards should treat the Indians. Naturally, many Spaniards said that his equal treatment of the Indians would bring the Spanish colonies to economic wreckage.

Las Casas made fourteen trips across the Atlantic Ocean to appeal his way to treat and win Indians. Because of his appeals, Charles V of Spain issued The Laws of the Indies, establishing greater human rights for Indians than before.

In Mexico Bartholomew was opposed in public debate by a Spanish theologian who argued: "The Spanish are as much above the Indians as man is above the ape." But in the 1550 debate Las Casas debated for the equality and freedom of the Indians. Like Paul, he wanted to view them not merely as "souls" to be won, but as humans of equal value.[13]

Two things can happen to class structure: (1) it can be transcended through Christ, or (2) it can tumble down because of Christ. The above paragraph illustrates the first phase.

While slavery has virtually been abolished, class distinctions still exist—according to levels of money made, education attained, status achieved, newspaper headlines secured, size of office desk held, etc. It's amazing the ways people try to put themselves "above" others—by name dropping, by having the right contacts, by worming into the "in" group, by buttering up the higher-ups, or by simply glancing away when approaching certain people.

Christianity transcends class distinctions. But until a person consciously identifies the subtle class and social distinctions of our day, he or she will probably not be conscious of treating people with different levels of importance. Take a quickie test: Do you treat secretaries as respectfully as you treat executives? Are you as courteous to the church custodian as you are to the pastor? Do you value blue-collar workers as highly as white-collar workers? How do you treat the person who picks up your garbage? As a farmer, do you look down on "city slickers"? As a city person, do you consider farmers "hicks"? Do you sometimes wish minority groups would disappear? Do you sometimes wish majority groups would disappear? These are the sort of questions verse 16 of Philemon forces us to face. Charles R. Brown commented that the proper answer to the question, "Am I my brother's keeper?" is "No, but you are your brother's brother [or sister]."[14]

Not only did Paul ground his appeal in Christian equality and human dignity (vs. 16), but beyond that he asked the slave master to "welcome him as you would welcome me" (vs. 17). What a jolt! Treat a slave as you would treat an apostle? A tall order!

CHRISTIANITY AND SOCIAL SITUATIONS

Throughout church history, Christians have been concerned with meeting social needs (cf. Gal. 2:10; Jas. 2:1-6, 15, 16; I Jn. 3:17). Here are some examples:

• "When Alexandria [Egypt] was devastated by plague in the . . . third century, Dionysius, bishop of the church in that city, describes the devotion with which Christians tended the sick, often catching the plague and dying of it . . . ."[15]

• John Calvin "diagrammed the sewer system for the city [of Geneva], codified its ordinances of Civil law, and helped establish the weaving industry in the city."[16]

• John Wesley set up the first free medical dispensary in England to help the poor of Bristol. His last letter, six days before his death, was written to encourage William Wilberforce in his fight to emancipate slaves.

• Charles Wesley lived in class-conscious England of the 1700s. Both he and George Whitefield (later to become a famous evangelist) attended the same university. George and Charles came from a different social class. Whitefield was a servitor at Pembroke College, which means he was a lackey, a flunky, to richer students. In exchange for free tuition he shined shoes, cleaned rooms, and ran errands. Because he was poor, he was segregated from the philosophical debates and Communion services of higher-ranked students.

Whitefield had longed to be part of the Holy Club, but school customs prohibited him from even talking with those students. Wesley, however, broke Oxford's rules and invited the social underling, Whitefield, to breakfast. They hit it off immediately, and George called Charles his "never-to-be-forgotten friend." Out of that meeting eventually came the greatest spiritual awakening England has ever known—all because Charles Wesley was willing to ignore the social class structure of his day.

• John Howard, influenced by John Wesley, was captured by a French privateer ship. He witnessed firsthand prison horrors. Consequently he "traveled 50,000 miles at home and abroad and spent $84,000 of his own money . . . to remedy this shocking state" of prisons.[17]

• The seventh Earl of Shaftesbury, who came to Christ through his housekeeper, introduced laws to revolutionize conditions in mental institutions, to improve the situation of factory workers, and to help prevent child labor in England.

- D. L. Moody helped provide food, clothing, and spiritual solace for the nearly 150,000 people rendered homeless by the Chicago fire of 1871.

Not only did a servant become a brother in the person of Onesimus, but in the person of Paul a creditor ("you owe me your very self," vs. 19) volunteered to become a debtor ("charge it to me," vs. 18). In verse 18 the apostle adopted the role of accountant. The beginning "if" in verse 18 is a special Greek construction (just as in vs. 17) that assumes the condition of the clause to be true and could even be translated "since." It is altogether likely that Onesimus had "done [Philemon] wrong" (vs. 18). He had probably skipped out of town and been A.W.O.L. for an indefinite period. Furthermore, he may have stolen something when making his getaway. If he had traveled by land and sea over a thousand miles to Rome from Colosse, funds were certainly required. Nevertheless, Paul mailed Philemon an IOU for Onesimus's debt. Philemon really owed Paul (vs. 19) much more than Onesimus owed Philemon.

An Allegorical Analogy

The verb translated "charge it to me" (vs. 18) is found only elsewhere in the New Testament at Romans 5:13 (translated "taken into account"). The story of Onesimus and Paul may be viewed as a parable of every Christian's experience. We have labored under a mountain of sin-debt. But Christ came, allowing our debt to be charged to Him (I Pet. 2:24). Also He passed on the credit card of His righteousness to us (II Cor. 5:21). Thus, we might place Paul's words in Jesus' mouth as they relate to our sin-debt: "charge it to me" (Philem. 18). Therefore, Christ's righteousness is counted as ours (Rom. 4:22-25).

 We are all the Lord's Onesimi.

—Martin Luther

So Long (19-25)

Perhaps Paul reached over with a manacled wrist and took the writing instrument. He penned: "I, Paul, am writing this with my own hand. I will pay it back . . ." (vs. 19). Some have surmised that Onesimus may not necessarily have stolen any sum, but simply may have overstayed a leave of absence from Philemon with Paul. If so, that would still seem to require the reimbursement Paul offers. Sir William Ramsay the archaeologist theorized that in later years Paul may have inherited some money from his family (note his loyal nephew in Acts 23:16) so as to be kept prisoner in "his own rented house" in Rome for two years

(Acts 28:30). At any rate, verse 19 functions, as it were, as Paul's enclosed *Visa* card.

Concerning verse 20 J. B. Lightfoot said: "It is the entreaty of a brother to a brother on behalf of a brother."[18] Paul makes another word play on the name of Onesimus in verse 20 when he says, "that I may have some benefit" (*onaimen* in Greek).

What did Philemon wind up doing? As Alexander Pushkin says at the end of one of his love stories: you finish the ending. Did they all "live happily ever after?" We don't know. Paul seemed "confident of your [i.e., Philemon's] obedience . . . knowing that you will do even more than I ask" (vs. 21).

The lionish British thinker Samuel Johnson once remarked: "More knowledge may be gained of a man's real character by a short conversation with one of his servants than from a formal and studied narrative, begun with his pedigree and ended with his funeral."[19]

What would Onesimus have said of Philemon? Interestingly, Ignatius of Antioch, an early church leader after the time of the apostles, wrote to a bishop of Ephesus named Onesimus. This later Onesimus may have been the very same slave!

Five of the ten individuals named in Colossians 4 are mentioned in verses 23 and 24 of Philemon. Why is Epaphras, presumably the founder-pastor of the Colossian church (Col. 1:7, 8; 4:12), called here a "fellow prisoner" with Paul (vs. 23)? Was this just a pictoral expression of loyalty, since it literally means "fellow prisoner of war" (the same title afforded Aristarchus elsewhere)? Or could it mean that Aristarchus and Epaphras were voluntarily taking turns in Paul's "rented" jail to serve the needs of the veteran apostle?

Presumably the four figures in verse 24 were free. Here the apostle mentions Mark and Luke, who (along with Paul) were responsible for writing about 60% of the New Testament.

 If you were to close a letter by paying compliments to Christians close to you, who would you name, how would you characterize them, and why?

Did "the grace of the Lord Jesus Christ" so mellow the "spirit" of Philemon (vs. 25) that he fully forgave and even freed the former fugitive? Apocryphal writers and novelists are more than willing to manufacture embellishing details that Scripture cloaks in silence. It leaves the question—and the quest—for us an open-ended one. What will we do with the Philemons that cross our path? How will I react if I am the Philemon of today?

The graciousness of our Lord Jesus Christ be with your spirit.

NOTES

Chapter 1
[1] Ralph Martin, *Colossians and Philemon* (London: Oliphants, 1974), p. 9.
[2] E. K. Simpson, *The Pastoral Epistles* (Grand Rapids, MI: Eerdmans, 1954), p. 1.
[3] Adolph Deissmann, *Light from the Ancient East* (Grand Rapids, MI: Baker, 1965),
    p. 179.

Chapter 2
[1] William Barnhart, *Christianity Today*, 31 July, 1970.
[2] C. F. D. Moule, *Colossians and Philemon* (Cambridge: Cambridge University Press,
    1962), p. 53.
[3] Herman Bavinck, *The Doctrine of God* (Grand Rapids, MI: Eerdmans, 1951), p. 195.
[4] *Antiquities of the Jews*, 9.235.
[5] A. T. Robertson, *Word Pictures in the New Testament, IV* (Nashville, TN: Broadman,
    1931), p. 480.

Chapter 3
[1] P. T. O'Brien, *Colossians, Philemon* (Waco, TX: Word, 1982), p. 66.
[2] O'Brien, Ibid., p. 68.
[3] A. T. Robertson, *Paul and the Intellectuals* (Nashville, TN: Broadman, 1956), p. 60.
[4] Ernst Kasemann, *Commentary on Romans* (Grand Rapids, MI: Eerdmans, 1980),
    p. 307.
[5] Lewis Johnson, *Bibliotheca Sacra*, July, 1962, p. 229.
[6] *Anabasis*, 1.2.18.

Chapter 4
[1] O'Brien, *Colossians*, p. xxix.
[2] William Hendriksen, *Colossians and Philemon* (Grand Rapids, MI: Baker, 1964),
    p. 120.
[3] Robertson, *Paul and the Intellectuals*, pp. 84, 85.
[4] Hendriksen, *Colossians and Philemon*, p. 20.
[5] Jess Moody, *The Jesus Freaks* (Waco, TX: Word Books, 1971), p. 45.

Chapter 5
[1] Robertson, *Paul and the Intellectuals*, p. 97.
[2] F. F. Bruce, *Commentary on the Epistles to the Ephesians and Colossians* (Grand Rapids,
    MI: Eerdmans, 1957), p. 258.
[3] James Denney, in Lewis Johnson, *Bibliotheca Sacra*, January, 1964.
[4] *The Interpreter's Bible, XI* (Nashville, TN: Abingdon, 1955), p. 212.
[5] Brian Dill, *Comprehensive Bible Study* (Elgin, IL: David C. Cook), February 22, 1987.
[6] Graham Kerr, *Christianity Today*, 12 June, 1981.
[7] Robertson, *Paul and the Intellectuals*, p. 101.
[8] Martin, *Colossians and Philemon*, p. 104.
[9] Hendriksen, *Colossians and Philemon*, p. 147.
[10] Dennis Guernsey, *The Family Covenant* (Elgin, IL: David C. Cook) p. 103.

Chapter 6
[1] O'Brien, *Colossians, Philemon*, p. 188.
[2] J. A. T. Robinson, *The Body* (London: S. C. M. Press, 1957), p. 31.
[3] Donald Guthrie, *The New Bible Commentary: Revised* (Grand Rapids, MI: Eerdmans,
    1970), p. 1150.

[4] IV. 64, 65.
[5] Moule, *Colossians and Philemon*, p. 212.
[6] James McNair, *Livingstone the Liberator* (London: House of Collins, 1940), p. 106.
[7] McNair, Ibid., p.101.
[8] John Knox, *Philemon Among the Letters of Paul* (Nashville: Abingdon, 1959), p. 35.
[9] in Lewis Johnson, *Bibliotheca Sacra*, January, 1964.

Chapter 7
[1] quoted in Edward Lohse, *Colossians and Philemon* (Philadelphia: Fortress, 1971), p. 155.
[2] quoted by Beare in *The Interpreter's Bible*, XI, p. 224, 225.
[3] Robertson, *Paul and the Intellectuals*, p. 118.
[4] John Eadie, *Commentary on the Epistle of Paul to the Colossians* (Grand Rapids, MI: Zondervan, 1957), p. 262.
[5] Catherine Stonehouse, *Patterns in Moral Development*, pp. 50, 57.
[6] William Barclay, *More New Testament Words* (New York: Harper and Brothers, 1958), p. 152.
[7] Beare, *The Interpreter's Bible*, IX, 320.
[8] Curtis Mitchell, *Christianity Today*, 16 September, 1983.
[9] Robertson, *Paul and the Intellectuals*, p. 129.
[10] Ronald Ward, *Royal Sacrament,* (London: Marshall, Morgan, and Scott, 1958), p. 67.

Chapter 8
[1] Leon Morris, *The Biblical Expositor*, III (Philadelphia: A. J. Holman, 1960), p. 330, 331.
[2] William Ramsay, *St. Paul the Traveller* (Grand Rapids, MI: Baker, 1962), pp. 315 ff.
[3] Robertson, *Paul and the Intellectuals*, p. 137.
[4] Beare, *The Interpreter's Bible*, XI, p. 238.
[5] Hendriksen, *Colossians and Philemon*, p. 13.
[6] Moule, *Colossians and Philemon*, p. 15.
[7] Robert Gundry, *A Survey of the New Testament* (Grand Rapids, MI: Zondervan, 1970), p. 31.
[8] Robertson, *Paul and the Intellectuals*, p. 143.

Chapter 9
[1] Martin, *Colossians and Philemon*, p. 9.
[2] Edgar Goodspeed, *An Introduction to the New Testament* (Chicago: University of Chicago Press, 1937), p. 107.
[3] Moule, *Colossians and Philemon*, p. 86.
[4] in William Barclay, *Jesus As They Saw Him* (New York: Harper and Row, 1962), p.79.
[5] Lewis Johnson, *Bibliotheca Sacra*, July, 1962.
[6] Martin, *Colossians and Philemon*, p. 79.
[7] Martin, Ibid., p. 92.

Chapter 10
[1] adapted from A. T. Robertson, *Word Pictures in the New Testament*, pp. iv, xvi, xvii.
[2] Martin, *Colossians and Philemon*, p. 14.
[3] Bruce, *Commentary on the Epistles to the Ephesians and Colossians*, p. 232.
[4] Hendriksen, *Colossians and Philemon*, pp. 111, 112.
[5] Hendriksen, Ibid., p. 76.

Chapter 11
[1] George Buttrick, *The Interpreter's Bible*, XI, p. 561.
[2] E. M. Blaiklock, *Commentary on the New Testament* (Old Tappan, NJ: Revell, 1977), p. 209.
[3] Buttrick, *The Interpreter's Bible*, XI, p. 561.

[4] Lohse, *Colossians and Philemon*, p. 176.

[5] Tim Dowley, ed., *Eerdman's Handbook to the History of Christianity* (Grand Rapids, MI: Eerdmans, 1977), p. 38.

[6] Hendriksen, *Colossians and Philemon*, p. 211.

[7] John Knox, *The Interpreters Bible*, XI, 563.

[8] Robertson, *Word Pictures*, IV, p. 465.

[9] Moule, *Colossians and Philemon*, p. 172.

[10] in O'Brien, *Colossians, Philemon*, p. 291.

Chapter 12

[1] J. W. Shepherd, *The Christ of the Gospels*, (Grand Rapids, MI: Eerdmans, 1939), p. xv.

[2] George Ladd, *Theology of the New Testament* (Grand Rapids, MI: Eerdmans, 1974), p. 529.

[3] Marvin Vincent, *Philippians and Philemon* (New York: Charles Scribner's Sons, 1906), p. 158.

[4] Ralph Martin, *New Testament Foundations*, II (Grand Rapids, MI: Eerdmans, 1978), p. 314.

[5] Charles Campbell, *Comprehensive Bible Study*, (Elgin, IL: David C. Cook).

[6] Hendriksen, *Colossians and Philemon*, p. 220.

[7] Buttrick, *The Interpreter's Bible*, XI, 569.

[8] Martin, *Colossians and Philemon*, p. 149.

[9] Beare, *The Interpreter's Bible*, XI, 229.

[10] From August Strindberg's play *Miss Julie*.

[11] quoted by Eduard Lohse, *Colossians and Philemon*, p. 203.

[12] quoted by Moule, *Colossians and Philemon*, p. 155.

[13] Bruce Shelley, *Church History in Plain Language* (Waco, TX: Word, 1982), pp. 302, 303.

[14] Buttrick, *The Interpreter's Bible*, XI, 571.

[15] F. F. Bruce, *The Spreading Flame* (Grand Rapids, MI: Eerdmans, 1958), p. 49.

[16] Bernard Ramm, *The Right, the Good and the Happy* (Waco, TX: Word, 1971), pp. 128, 129.

[17] Herbert Lockyer, *The Man Who Changed the World*, II (Grand Rapids, MI: Zondervan, 1966), p. 136.

[18] J. B. Lightfoot, *Saint Paul's Epistles to the Colossians and to Philemon* (Grand Rapids, MI: Zondervan, 1961), p. 344.

[19] Wayne Warner, *1000 Stories and Quotations of Famous People* (Grand Rapids, MI: Baker, 1975), p. 167.

DIRECTIONS FOR GROUP LEADERS

The questions and projects should form the framework of the actual time spent in group discussion. The week before every class the leader ought to assign both the lesson and the Bible passage (found under each chapter title) to be read for the upcoming class so that students will come to class with an informational foundation for the discussion.

Some class members may come without having read the lesson for the week. It would be wise to have a plan for including them in a short review session before jumping into the study proper. Perhaps two or three other class members could give an "overview report" with highlights from the reading. Certain portions of the book could be read aloud. Or, you could set up a short dialogue session between two who have read the lesson content. However you do it, make sure the unprepared members feel every bit as important to the class as the others.

The New International Version, 1984 edition, is the Bible translation quoted throughout the commentary, although the study can be conducted using any helpful translation. Remember to read the directions for each chapter at least a week before class. That way, you will have adequate time to pull together some of the special learning experiences requiring advance preparation.

To encourage group discussion, don't be shy about asking, "Susan, in what ways has this issue been a part of your own life experience?" If someone responds to a question, you can add something like, "How have others of you dealt with this?"

Don't be afraid of respectful disagreement, for we can learn from people who differ from us. Even if you don't agree, you can comment, 'I don't think I agree, but it will certainly give us something to think about. How do others of you feel?" The secret of effective group discussion is to keep throwing open-ended questions (*not* questions that can be answered with a mere "yes" or "no") *back* to members of the group. Be sure to acknowledge people's contributions: 'Thanks for sharing that, David. I know it took some courage to bring that up."

Try to include in all your group sessions some of the key ingredients for building group life: a time for sharing, a time for prayer, and perhaps light refreshments around which significant conversation can take place. Bible study groups can be much more that just an intellectual trip. They can become a means of developing strong bonds of Christian fellowship.

Below, three items will be found for each of the 12 class sessions:

A. Need-hook. Each week this paragraph will provide a discussion item with which to open class. Normally it will try to hook into some felt need humans experience that will in turn tie into a major truth emerging from the Bible passage to be studied. Hence, the leader moves the class from a felt need to the Bible principles.

B. Fun Feature(s). Every week the leader is provided with an activity (to do or discuss) with an element of group action or even humor involved. This group game or project will sensitize the students to an idea or issue from the particular passage being studied.

C. For Group Discussion. While there are usually a number of questions included within the body of the commentary at pertinent points in the flow of the study, seven to ten extra application questions on each given Bible passage are supplied here. The leader should allow plenty of time for students to think about and respond to the questions. If all questions and activities are used, the class time will probably take about an hour (although by selectivity in the use of the questions, the class time could be made shorter).

Happy study and good grouping to you!

CHAPTER 1

A. A Need-hook

1. Suppose you had a cousin who was flirting with involvement in a cult. Have students take a small piece of paper and start a letter to him or her (no more than 10 lines).

(After students read some of their openers to the imaginary cousin, note how Paul does not even mention the threat of the cult in his opener to the Colossians. Let students speculate as to why.)

2. Can you recall some letter or memo that gave you an emotional pickup? In essence, what was said to you? What do you see in Colossians 1:1-9 that might lift Christians' spirits and establish rapport?

B. Fun Features.

1. Write out and make copies of the geographical and historical fill-in-the-blank section at the first part of chapter one and let students

cluster in threes to look up the Bible references and answer the background questions.

2. Let students select small groups according to their preferences and compile lists of information about various cults. Later, share the information in turn.

C. For Group Discussion

1. How many things can you remember as a group about Colossians before beginning this study?

2. Can you cite an example about someone having an unhealthy or dangerous view of the human body? After polling students, read aloud the six items on page 12 and see if students can amplify or illustrate these examples any further.

3. What image do you have of a "holy" person (1:2)? Do you think this image is out of kilter or is it an attractive one?

4. What strikes you from Colossians 1:3-6 about the way Paul addressed people who were susceptible to approaches from a cult?

5. What is one way the "hope that is stored up for you in heaven" (1:5) motivates you or supplies some concrete need in your life now?

6. What spin-off implications can you think of from the fact that the Gospel is called "the word of *truth*" (1:5)?

7. What specific way can you name that the Gospel has been "bearing fruit" (1:6) in your life or that of someone else you know since the point of belief?

8. If you could have a mature, personal counselor (of the sort that Epaphras appears to have been in 1:7), what characteristics would your "Epaphras" possess?

CHAPTER 2

A. A Need-hook

1. You've prayed for all of one minute and exhausted your list of requests, right? What should a Christian pray for?

Let students brainstorm concerning what Paul prayed for in Colossians 1:9-11, suggesting what tips Paul's written prayer might suggest for their own particular friends.

2. Benjamin Franklin once stated in a letter, "As to Jesus of Nazareth, . . . I have some doubts as to his Divinity . . ." (in Bruce Shelley, *Church History in Plain Language*, p. 329). How might you respond to Franklin from Colossians 1:15-20? Would you add any Bible passages? Discuss.

B. Fun Feature

Let each student write out on an index card a commercial for a make-believe modern cult called Knowists. These Knowists are heady people who lure people by their mind games, their stress on intellectualism. Let students volunteer to read their commercials to the group. Then move to Colossians 1:9, observing which words would zero in on Knowists' interests.

C. For Group Discussion

1. What are some realistic techniques you can think of for (shall we say) nonstop praying (Col. 1:9) for certain individuals?

2. Can you flash back to one time when you feel that you applied "spiritual wisdom" (1:9) to some delicate or difficult situation? What did it involve? Can you think of an example of having knowledge without using wisdom?

3. Colossians 1:10 encourages us to "please him [God] in every way." In what one way or area do you desire to please God more?

4. Name one person who has shown "great endurance and patience" (1:11). How did you witness those qualities being manifested in that person?

5. Colossians 1:11 speaks of joyfulness. Do you think some people are just naturally happier than others? How do you think joy grows?

6. What does "the forgiveness of sins" (1:14) mean to you personally?

7. Many scholars think Colossians 1:15-20 was an early Christian hymn. What do hymns do for you? Do you have a hymn or hymn line that is meaningful to you? If so, what and why?

8. How would you feel if you were God (who desires "to reconcile to himself all things" [1:19]) looking at our world? Can anything be done to change this situation? What do you feel is your part in it?

CHAPTER 3

A. A Need-hook

"I've Got a Secret" used to be the name of an early TV program. Pass out pencils and small pieces of paper. Let all class members write down on paper some deep, dark (probably funny) secret about themselves (e.g., "I used to work on an assembly line in a pickle packing plant"). After the "secrets" have been turned over to you, read each secret aloud. As you read each secret, ask for a show of hands, allowing class participants to guess who the "secret" person is.

(Each person should keep a count of how many actually guess his or her secret correctly. The one whose secret gets the least correct guesses wins whatever "secret" prize you award.)

From that activity move to the "mystery" or secret (1:28; 2:2) which is the heart of Colossians 1:21—2:7.

B. Fun Feature

Phone class members ahead of time asking each one to bring an old snapshot (as a baby, child, or teenager). If you wish, you could display the photographs and allow all to guess who is who.

Comment that these photos provide us with a "before." Divide the class into small groups and let them discuss any "before" and "after" features (1:21, 22) of their becoming Christians. Perhaps few will be of the dramatic "Damascus Road" type, so people will be forced to think about what particular changes Christ is bringing them.

C. For Group Discussion

1. Would you share a time when you felt "alienated" (1:21) from some individual or group? How can that experience help you in relating to non-Christians?

2. What aspect of Christian experience do you find most difficult for you as you "continue in your faith" (1:23)?

3. Can you think of an example of someone who has "suffered" (1:24) for someone else or one who has suffered for his or her faith?

4. Paul's methods involved "admonishing and teaching" (1:28). What creative methods (and specific examples) can you name that Christians have used effectively to make Christ known?

5. Read the stories of Steve and Jeanette from the chapter aloud. Can you think of any other examples of false passivism or activism (related to 1:29)?

6. How do you think Paul's expression of "struggling" (2:1) relates to modern ideas like "the victorious Christian life"?

7. Can you think of anyone you've influenced positively whom you "have not met . . . personally" (2:1)?

8. Do you think that people who think very differently from you can be "united in love" (2:2) with you?

CHAPTER 4

A. A Need-hook

1. If you have several group "hams," get two ahead of class to work

134

up a skit—with one being the "all-positive" enlightened sophisticate and the other being the "tied-up-in-don'ts" person. They should talk about some subject with the one sounding all positive and the other all negative.

Tie in the skit with the Colossian cultists who manifested some of both of these characteristics—parading their philosophy that claimed to possess sophisticated "fullness" (2:9), yet shunning many physical privileges because of negative regulations (see "do not" in 2:21).

2. Ask the class, "Would you share some occasion when you discovered that you had been deceived?" Tie this discussion to Colossians 2:8.

B. Fun Features

1. Dress up like a pirate and make up a skit that will tie in piracy with parallels to (1) carrying off booty—see notes on 2:8; (2) treasure—2:3; (3) the danger lurking at Colosse (2:8, 16-23); etc.

2. Let students do brief research from encyclopedias or library books (before or during class) on Captain Kidd, Blackbeard, Henry Morgan, Sir Francis Drake and other famous pirates. See how many ways you can tie this in with the philosophical pirates (2:8) and Christian treasure (2:3) in Colossians.

C. For Group Discussion

1. Can you recall any form of thinking or idea you have been exposed to that you came to conclude was "hollow" (2:8)? (If you have any students familiar with existentialist philosophers' writings, you might see if they can recall passages or find quotes on emptiness.)

2. Pass out hymnbooks. What hymns can you find that reveal an exalted view of Christ's deity, such as is found in 2:9?

3. In what ways are you finding "fullness in Christ" (2:10)?

4. How would you rewrite Colossians 2:16 so as to update it?

5. Can you give any recent examples of "false humility" (2:18, 23)?

6. Do you feel that your church body realistically represents the latter part of Colossians 2:19? If not, how might it more accurately do so?

7. Can you think of modern examples of excessive negativism (cp. 2:21)? Share and discuss.

8. Can you think of any religious "harsh treatment of the body" (2:23)? (You may wish to read aloud the three examples at the conclusion of the study guide's chapter.) Do these methods appear to have "any value in restraining sensual indulgence" (2:23)?

CHAPTER 5

A. A Need-hook

Wouldn't it be wonderful to be able to take a hatchet or machete and hack away specific sins in the same way a jungle explorer chops away vines? Ask the class: how do you think a Christian should cope with specific sinful habits? Do you think non-Christian Benjamin Franklin's habit of keeping a diary to check off days when he didn't commit a certain vice is acceptable or unchristian?

B. Fun Features

1. Bring in ample cardboard. Let students divide into pairs and have each pair come up with three placards that read: "Down with . . . ." They may fill in the blank with actual historical examples they recall or ones they might wish to see.

After all have displayed their placards, see if any have made one that reads: "Down with Sin." After all, that's pretty basic—and it gets right at the subject of 3:5-8.

2. Pass out pencil and paper to each student. In groups of three, let them write out working, down-to-earth definitions of the ten sins listed in 3:5 and 8. Also, the small group should name one illustration of how people today may commit each of these sins.

C. For Group Discussion

1. How would you answer the skeptic who asks: "How on earth could the dying and (as you Christians claim) rising of this Jesus possibly have anything to say about office politics or stopping alcoholism or arrogance?"

2. What would you say to someone who claimed, "Carrying out Colossians 3:1, 2 makes a person too heavenly minded to be any earthly good"? Can you give an illustration of the misapplication of these verses?

3. Do you see any interrelationship between or progression among the five sins named in 3:5?

4. How can a Christian be guilty of "greed" (3:5)? Would you volunteer a time when you felt guilt feelings about possible greed?

5. In what sense could the five sins in 3:5 be labeled "idolatry"?

6. Read the illustration by Dennis Guernsey from the study manual. Does becoming a Christian mean that instantaneously all bad habits fall off (as some interpret II Cor. 5:17)? How might you have been helped more as a new Christian by older Christians?

7. Is a Christian to get rid of all anger (3:8)? What verses support your position?

8. Suppose a new believer confesses to you that he's having a terrible time with his old habit of "filthy language" (3:8). What could you suggest to him?

CHAPTER 6

A. A Need-hook

Read aloud the following poem:

> I dream of a land called the
>   Land of Beginning Again,
> Where all our mistakes
>   And all our heartaches
> Could be dropped like a
>   shabby old coat at the door
> And never put on anymore.

See if some class member is willing to open up and talk about some habit that he or she wishes could be burned up once and for all (as the poem indicates).

Move then to the image of character clothing in 3:9, 10.

B. Fun Feature

Divide into groups of 2-4 with a person recording notes. Each group studies the eight items of character clothing found in 3:12-14. Let students have fun by creatively matching each virtue with an appropriate item of clothing. For example, some might liken "humility" to a work apron, "gentleness" to a protective sun hat, "love" to a nurse's uniform, etc.

After brainstraining, look at page 64 to see the author's portrayal. (P.S. In *Buried Treasure in Colossians,* a multimedia learning kit from the same author and publisher, you will find an overhead transparency of this exercise to show your class.)

C. For Group Discussion

1. How do you reconcile 3:9 with 3:5 (that we should "put to death" sins if already we "have taken off" the "old self with its practices")?

2. Can you think of some way in which you have felt "renewed" (3:10) as a Christian within the past year? What would you say to a fellow believer who says to you, "What should I do to be renewed?"

3. What is one way you have seen the principle of 3:11 applied within your local church?

4. Name one Christian who shows "compassion" or "kindness" (3:12). How have you seen that quality manifested?

5. Make a group list of specific forms that "compassion" could take among people of your acquaintance.

6. How would you respond to a believer who says, "I keep trying to forgive so-and-so (3:13), but my mind just keeps bringing up the wrong she did?"

7. What are two things you are "thankful" (3:15) for? What is one unpleasant thing that—in retrospect—you're now thankful for?

CHAPTER 7

A. A Need-hook

1. Read aloud the contrasting family illustrations of David Livingstone and Marilyn Monroe under "Windows on the Word." Ask class members to share particular ways they have witnessed Christianity impacting a home for good.

2. Ask the class if they can cite particular illustrations of how Christianity *seems* to have impeded society's progress or has been a negative influence on culture. Why may these instances have existed? Can you think of such situations that may presently exist? How does Colossians 3:18—4:6 bear upon these issues?

B. Fun Feature

Divide the class into threesomes. Let each threesome write an update to some of Paul's basic strata of society: (For example, "Pastors, don't manipulate or dominate your congregations." Or, "Parents, don't let your teenagers throw you out of joint.") After the writing exercise, let each group share their written results.

C. For Group Discussion

1. Do you think Paul meant 3:18 as a burdensome command? How do you understand it in light of Galatians 3:28? Do you think Colossians 3:18 is compatible with feminism? If so or if not, why?

2. What are various ways that a husband might "be harsh" (3:19) toward his wife?

3. Suppose a child is abused. Would 3:20 still apply? Is "in everything" to be qualified? At what age do you think this command might no longer apply?

4. What are some forms of child rearing that you think might leave a child with embitterment (3:21)? How might the bitterness of an adult daughter who was sexually abused by her father in a Christian home be alleviated?

5. If both children (3:20) and slaves (3:22) are told to "obey . . . in everything," does that reduce children to the level of slaves? Do you think there are occasions for disobedience? If you think so, for what and why?

6. What area of your life might you need encouragement to "work at it with all your heart" (3:23)?

7. How can an employer determine standards by which to pay "what is right and fair" (4:1)?

8. How many tips can you list from 4:2-6 about how to engage in effective evangelism?

CHAPTER 8

A. A Need-hook

Ask class members to think of some fairly incidental comment or action by someone that helped them feel affirmed (e.g., "he jumped to his feet to shake hands with me"). Let as many individuals as can think of an example of being affirmed share their responses. From the sharing time move to 4:7-18 where Paul affirms or compliments people, sometimes simply by mentioning their names.

B. Fun Feature

Since this week winds up your passage-by-passage study of Colossians, you can do as a class essentially what Paul did at the conclusion of Colossians. Have students imitate this passage by writing notes to each other in which they mention any qualities they cherish in their classmates (e.g., "I am sending you greetings from Netta, whose transparency I value greatly and who bakes a first class coffee cake"). If you have 12 students or less (and they've had adequate chance to get acquainted), each person should be able to write a note of appreciation to every other person. If the group is larger, figure out a way to do this exercise without leaving anyone out.

C. For Group Discussion

1. Paul describes Tychicus in three ways in 4:7. Who is one believer whom you can compliment in three appreciative ways?

2. Would you have trusted an ex-runaway slave with your inside information (4:9)? What can Paul's attitude here teach us?

3. The word "comfort" (4:11) is the Greek word from which we get the name of the medicine *paregoric*. In what way might you act as a medicine for someone you know this week? What medicine label would you attach to one of your close friends (e.g., "Dale is my alka seltzer. He supplies a lot of fizz in my life.")?

4. Whom would you name as having "proved" (4:11) himself or herself to you in a time of critical need?

5. How might you help a believer with little confidence come to feel more "fully assured" (4:12)?

6. Luke had particular professional skills (4:14) dedicated to God. Who would you name as having professional skills dedicated to God, and how does that person use his or her vocation for God?

7. Paul was writing under less-than-ideal circumstances (4:18). What Christian do you know laboring under difficult circumstances, and how could you and your group assist that person?

CHAPTER 9

A. A Need-hook

Which of the following items do you think constitutes the greatest threat to your church?

    (a) doctrinal questions
    (b) personality frictions, cliques
    (c) lack of financial sacrifice
    (d) lethargy, uninvolvement
    (e) personality dominance
    (f) lack of know-how in skills or training
    (g) insufficient outreach
    (h) other

How do you think that need can be more effectively met?

From there move to the study guide's discussion of the threat at Colosse and reason for the letter being written.

B. Fun Feature

Check your local (or pastor's) library to see if you can find a book (or several)—religious, theological, philosophical, or cultish)that is written in language that almost no one can really understand. After reading some excerpts from this intellectual gobbledygook, talk about the intellectual-sounding cult at Colosse (combatted by full "knowledge," 1:9, 10; a genuine "mystery," 1:26, 27; 2:2, etc.).

C. For Group Discussion

1. What do you remember most about our study of Colossians? What practical application from it do you find useful?

2. Can you think of any philosophy or modern religious group that Colossians might oppose? How?

3. In light of religious cults and false ideas, how can a Christian stand firm without being overly defensive, intolerant, or unloving?

4. If you had to summarize what the Bible's view of "knowledge" (1:9, 10) is, what would you say in a few sentences?

5. What might be some modern examples of giving undue veneration to angels?

6. What implications might we derive from Paul's emphasis upon "everyone" (twice in 1:28)?

7. Suppose an advertisement appeared in a magazine, reading: "You cannot understand the Bible without these special books. They reveal the hidden secrets of life to you." How might you evaluate this in light of Colossians?

8. What are some ways that people (even some Christians) try (to borrow C. S. Lewis's phrase) "to be more spiritual than God"?

9. Are you familiar with any falsely spiritual attempts at conducting family life? Describe them.

CHAPTER 10

A. A Need-hook

Pick out three fairly articulate people (whom you may wish to contact ahead of time) to share with the class what they were like—and how they changed in their thinking—at three different phases of their lives (say, as a child, teenager, and adult).

After the three have told about different installments in their life, move to an explanation (from the first part of chapter 10 in the study guide) of this week's approach to Bible study—a Biblical theology (or topical approach) of Colossians. One radical starting point might be to contrast Psalm 137:8, 9 with Matthew 5:44—to show that there is a progression of the parts of revelation within the Bible.

B. Fun Feature

Let groups of three each select a topic (music, names, toys, customs, cars, TV shows, etc.) in which they think they can show how a number of items build upon a number of previous items in history. For instance, the "names" group of three might list: (1) George

Washington Carver based on George Washington's name (2) Martin Luther King deriving from Martin Luther, (3) John Quincy Adams is a progression from John Adams, etc.

Let each group share its findings after time is up. Then observe that in this week's study we are trying to see whether in Colossians Paul is building on any earlier doctrine or is giving teaching material that is only found in this letter.

C. For Group Discussion

1. What do you think are the pros and cons of a Christian's interest in doctrine?

2. Let groups of three scan Colossians 1. What could we safely say about God if all we had of the Bible was Colossians?

3. What may we learn about angels from 1:16; 2:10, 15, and 18?

4. Read aloud John 1:1-3; Philippians 2:6-11; Colossians 1:15-20 and 2:9; and Hebrews 1:1-4. Divide into groups of three and answer: What things do each of these passages teach in common about Christ (if anything)? Secondly, are there any distinctive teachings about Christ that are found only in any one of the passages?

5. Compare Ephesians 3:1-11 with Colossians 1:25-27 and 2:2, 3. How would you compare and contrast the two passages?

6. What do we learn about the opposing "cult" from Colossians 2:16-23? Divide into two or three groups, and let each group list as much as they know about some modern cult.

7. Let groups of four answer: "How would you state the practical lessons of 3:15-17 in your own words?"

CHAPTER 11

A. A Need-hook

On a chart, tablet, or large piece of paper write out the phrases:

"across the tracks"
bank presidents
welfare coupons
mink furs
no dandelions in the front yard
Ph.D.s
jet set
"keeping up with the Joneses"
ghetto
school dropout
three-piece suit

With little guidance, let your class make comments on the expressions. Then ask what the phrases say about our society. Observe that they say something about the way we categorize people—socially, economically, etc. From that point move to study Philemon and Onesimus, who were poles apart on the social spectrum, yet Christianity had some surprising implications for them.

B. Fun Feature

Bring in a stack of magazines with pictures. (You may need to call others to help you collect them.) Let students pair up and see how many pictures they can find (sticking markers in pages) that speak loudly about various social levels. After sharing these, the group can comment about how a Christian might relate to these various social cross sections.

C. For Group Discussion

1. If you had to update Paul's "grace . . . and peace" (vs. 3) for a catchy TV commercial to show people today the value of those virtues, how would you word these qualities?

2. Read Samuel Rutherford's quotation to the class. Do you think the experience of a Rutherford (or Corrie ten Boom in a Nazi camp) is realistic? Should every Christian be expected to respond that positively? On what do you base your answer?

3. Paul thanks God for Philemon (vss. 4, 5). For whom do you thank God? (P.S. How about dropping that person a thank-you note this week?)

4. What are five ways Christians can "be active in sharing [their] faith" (vs. 6)?

5. Verse 6 mentions "every good thing we have in Christ." (It's brainstorm time.) How many good things can you name that "we have in Christ"?

6. Paul says in verse 7: "Your love has given me great joy." About whom would you say that? Why? Who might say that about you? (No *false* humility, please!)

7. Can you remember a time when you felt that softening your approach (vs. 8) would be more effective than coming down hard?

CHAPTER 12

A. A Need-hook

Dave, a Christian from California who develops businesses, told about an employee who worked for him. The particular woman was both Jewish and a lesbian. She mentioned to Dave that she felt he had made unchristian or unkind comments in staff meetings about several groups. Rather than being offended or sulking, Dave invited her to check in weekly with him for a month on whether he was improving in his remarks. While the woman did not become a Christian, she was floored at Dave's sensitivity and willingness to change.

Can you think of any examples of how Christianity has brought about a turn of events that causes a "rewiring" of relationship? (From this discussion move to the same idea in the commentary.)

B. Fun Features

1. Phone two dramatic people ahead of time to act out a skit for the class involving some gap between social classes.

2. Hand out cutout cardboard pictures of bridges. Let groups of four come up with one Christian way they would want to see a bridge built up between two very different groups today. Write these ideas on the cutouts. One representative from each group should share their ideas with the total class.

C. For Group Discussion

In his Letter to Philemon Paul engages in a masterpiece of persuasion. What tips do you see? At what point do you think persuasion becomes manipulation? Can you give some examples of manipulative persuasion?

2. Keith Miller testified that one measurable change that he felt he should make as a Christian was to break with his old Southern family upbringing about what men should do and consequently to take out the garbage. In light of verse 11, can you think of some concrete change in behavior you or someone else has made that might symbolize a conversion?

3. John Wilson, a Durham, England, miner in the 1800s, said after his conversion to Christ: "This change made, I began seriously to consider how I could *be useful* in life." With what examples would you defend Christianity's usefulness (vs. 11)?

4. How would you apply the idea in verse 14—"I did not want to do anything without your consent"?

5. Can you think of some relationship restored through Christ despite past rifts and tensions (cf. vss. 15, 16)? What happened?

6. Can you think of an occasion when your friendship with one person (vs. 17) changed your attitude toward another person? Share.

7. Have you ever felt you had to ask someone to do something difficult (vss. 15-20) based on Christian principles? What happened?